LONGING,
WAITING,
BELIEVING

Published by
The Bible Reading Fellowship
15 The Chambers, Vineyard
Abingdon OX14 3FE
United Kingdom
Tel: +44 (0)1865 319700
Email: enquiries@brf.org.uk
Website: www.brf.org.uk
BRF is a Registered Charity

ISBN 978 1 84101 756 3
First published 2014
10 9 8 7 6 5 4 3 2 1 0

Acknowledgements
Unless otherwise stated, scripture quotations are taken from The New Revised
Standard Version of the Bible, Anglicised edition, copyright © 1989, 1995 by the
Division of Christian Education of the National Council of the Churches of Christ
in the United States of America, and are used by permission. All rights reserved.

Extracts from the Authorised Version of the Bible (The King James Bible), the
rights in which are vested in the Crown, are reproduced by permission of the
Crown's Patentee, Cambridge University Press.

Cover photo: Wise men: Robert Churchill/iStock; background: Milaneres/iStock/
Thinkstock

Every effort has been made to trace and contact copyright owners for material
used in this resource. We apologise for any inadvertent omissions or errors, and
would ask those concerned to contact us so that full acknowledgement can be
made in the future.

A catalogue record for this book is available from the British Library

Printed and bound by CPI Group (UK) Ltd, Croydon CR0 4YY

LONGING, WAITING, BELIEVING

REFLECTIONS FOR ADVENT, CHRISTMAS AND EPIPHANY

RODNEY HOLDER

Copyright Acknowledgements

Contents

Introduction

Advent is a time of looking forward, both to Christmas and to the consummation of all things when creation is renewed, humans are raised from the dead and Christ's reign becomes manifest and universal. It is a time of longing for God to act, waiting patiently for him to do so and believing that he will. For the Old Testament patriarchs and prophets, this longing and waiting lasted many centuries. The patriarchs heard God's call and followed, believing his promises that through them 'all the families on earth would be blessed' (Genesis 12:3). The visions and dreams of the prophets were fulfilled at best partially in their own lifetimes, but when those visions were fulfilled in their awesome reality it was in the most startling and unexpected way.

The history of this chosen people, the apple of God's eye, was one of stark contrasts between triumph and disaster. They won great victories and freedom from oppression but also endured slavery and exile. Their history eventually focused down on a small town in Judea where their dreams were finally realised. But fulfilment came not in the triumphant military victory of their long-awaited King-Messiah over their enemies. It came in a child born in obscurity who ended up 'despised and rejected' (Isaiah 53:3).

The child born that first Christmas was first revealed to the lowliest in Jewish society. Those who were longing and waiting for him included the old people Anna and Simeon, and those who believed in him were the humble—the carpenter Joseph and his teenage fiancée, Mary. Mary's 'Yes' to God is a model for our own 'Yes' to being part of God's purposes for the world.

The first visitors to the stable were shepherds, themselves despised because their occupation made them unable to participate in the religious rituals of their fellows. They believed and rejoiced in what they had been privileged to witness. The child Jesus was then revealed to Eastern sages, symbolising the availability of the gospel to all people. What dim awareness from their studies of the heavens prompted them to journey so far? Did they realise that this was the Saviour born to redeem the whole world—God's gift of his very self for all humanity? Who knows? Yet their role in the drama was also heralded many centuries before by the Old Testament writers.

As we journey through Advent, we hear the ever more urgent call to repent, to turn our lives round so that we are ready to meet the one who is to be both Saviour and Judge of the world. Many, including God's own people, long for justice, but do they realise that judgement begins with the household of God? (1 Peter 4:17). And if the standard we are required to measure up to is that of Christ himself, 'then who can be saved?' (Mark 10:26). In Advent we reflect on the four 'last things': death, judgement, heaven and hell. Is our destiny beyond death to be eternal life with Christ or the pains of hell? We worry about the destiny of others, but what of ourselves? The great good news of the gospel is that 'in all these things we are more than conquerors through him who loved us' (Romans 8:37). God's offer of mercy, forgiveness and new abundant life is made to the worst of sinners.

The call to repent was made most urgently by John the Baptist, yet he—Jesus' cousin and the prophesied forerunner to the Messiah—had doubts while languishing in Herod's prison fortress of Machaerus. He was reassured when his disciples witnessed to the mighty deeds that Jesus was doing before their eyes, but he was still beheaded (Matthew 11:2–6; 14:3–11). Just as John suffered for his faith and for speaking God's truth to the powerful, so it is the lot of Jesus' disciples to suffer for their faith. Having welcomed the Saviour, and in the midst of our Christmas festivities, we are immediately reminded of the first martyr, Stephen (26 December). Human brutality is to the fore as we also commemorate the slaughter of the innocents by Herod (28 December). We think about living in the 'now and not yet', the time when Jesus' followers, like their Master, will be hated and persecuted. Yet we who believe have been left the great resources of word and sacrament and the Holy Spirit to empower us for his service: 'And remember, I am with you always, to the end of the age' (Matthew 28:20).

My thoughts on these themes reflect my background as a scientist. One of my heroes is John Polkinghorne, who was Professor of Mathematical Physics at Cambridge before training for ordination in the Church of England. Polkinghorne is fond of saying that science and theology bear a cousinly relationship to one another because they are both truth-seeking. Another hero is Georges Lemaître, the Roman Catholic priest who was 'Father of the Big Bang theory'. Lemaître once said, 'There were two ways of arriving at the truth. I decided to follow them both.' He meant, like Polkinghorne, science and theology.

Not every passage of scripture lends itself to a scientific approach, just as not every question we might want to ask is a scientific question. Whereas science is concerned with the processes of nature, theology is concerned with the much more fundamental questions of human existence. Why are we here? Where are we heading? What are the purpose and meaning of life? What is God's plan for the world and for our own individual lives? Nevertheless, there are many areas of interaction between science and theology and these disciplines can be mutually supportive.

My scientific mindset leads me to ask, when appropriate, 'What happened? What are the facts relating to this passage of scripture? What evidence do we have?' I have a profound respect for biblical scholarship, just as I have for scientific research. It seems to me that biblical scholarship aids our understanding, and hence our devotions, immensely, not least by helping us understand the context in which the various books of the Bible were written.

Another hero of mine is the German theologian and martyr Dietrich Bonhoeffer. Bonhoeffer's theology was forged in the tumultuous years of the Nazi tyranny in Germany. An opponent of the régime, he lived out his own central tenet of 'responsible action in obedience to Christ' to the point of martyrdom. He brings many insights to our journey of faith. My prayer, as we travel together this Advent, Christmas and Epiphany, is that our longing for Christ will be fulfilled, our waiting for him rewarded and our believing in him strengthened:

I pray that you may have the power to comprehend, with all the saints, what is the breadth and length and height and depth, and to know the love of Christ that surpasses knowledge, so that you may be filled with all the fullness of God. (Ephesians 3:18–19)

Preparation

I have used the New Revised Standard Version of the Bible throughout this book, but of course you may use any version of the Bible as an alternative.

On some days I have suggested that your reflection time might include listening or singing along to some music. So, unless you prefer simply to use the words for prayer, it would be good to have a CD player, tablet or other device handy, and, if you can get hold of them, recordings of the recommended music.

1–6 DECEMBER

Following God's call

Our Advent journey will take us from the distant past to the unknown future. It begins with the urgent call to 'wake from sleep' since 'the day is near'—but how near? It could be centuries away, but it could be tomorrow. Shall we be ready to meet the Lord? We must prepare ourselves by fulfilling the law, summed up in the command to love, and by putting off what is shameful and worldly.

The story of our salvation begins with the patriarchs. We are transported back two millennia to the time when God calls Abraham to uproot himself and journey into the unknown. Through Abraham's family, God plans to bless all the families of the earth. He will be faithful to his promise, despite the many failings of the human agents in this great drama.

Time to wake from sleep

Owe no one anything, except to love one another; for the one who loves another has fulfilled the law. The commandments, 'You shall not commit adultery; You shall not murder; You shall not steal; You shall not covet'; and any other commandment, are summed up in this word, 'Love your neighbour as yourself.' Love does no wrong to a neighbour; therefore, love is the fulfilling of the law.

Besides this, you know what time it is, how it is now the moment for you to wake from sleep. For salvation is nearer to us now than when we became believers; the night is far gone, the day is near. Let us then lay aside the works of darkness and put on the armour of light; let us live honourably as in the day, not in revelling and drunkenness, not in debauchery and licentiousness, not in quarrelling and jealousy. Instead, put on the Lord Jesus Christ, and make no provision for the flesh, to gratify its desires.

ROMANS 13:8–14

It is appropriate to begin our Advent journey with the overpowering sense of urgency that this passage presents to us. The Messiah is coming; we are to give an account of ourselves; we are to be judged; the day is at hand. Perhaps this night our life will be demanded of us. Are we about to face death or, alternatively, life in all its fullness for eternity? It is decision time. What shall we be found doing when the Master comes? Shall we, like the rich fool, be building ever bigger barns for our material goods (Luke 12:16–21)? Will the Master come suddenly and find us asleep, or shall we be on the watch because we do not know when he will come? (Mark 13:35–37). Shall we, as in today's passage, be caught in wanton and licentious behaviour or shall we be fulfilling the command to love?

Such questions haunted St Augustine, who was converted to Christ on reading this passage. While sitting in a garden in Milan, he heard the voice of a child saying, 'Take it and read; take it and read.' He remembered how St Antony had happened to go into a church and heard Matthew 19:21 read as the Gospel passage for the day: 'Go, sell your possessions, and give the money to the poor, and you will have treasure in heaven; then come, follow me.' Antony had taken that verse to be directly and literally aimed at himself, and acted on it. Might not the same happen for Augustine, he wondered, if he opened the scriptures at random?

It is not a method I would recommend in general for seeking God's direction for our lives, but, by God's providence, it worked for Augustine, just as it had for Antony. The passage Augustine lighted on was Romans 13:13–14.

Augustine realised that it was now or never. He had deceived himself long enough. He had been held back by his love of sexual pleasures, famously praying in his youth, 'Give me chastity and continence, but not yet.' Now he realised how preposterous that prayer was, and that such base and shameful desires were trivial in comparison with the joy of salvation and eternal life with Christ. He was also convinced of the truth of the Christian faith and the certainty of its hope.

Sin and temptation are real. They are very attractive to us and very hard to resist. God forbids the lusts of the flesh because they are harmful to us and to others. So can we really give up an eternity of bliss in the kingdom of God for a life of fleeting pleasures? My scientific training in using reason and evidence makes me want to take the rational course, although that does not mean my will is always able to do so. But pause and reflect. Surely it is far, far better to come to Christ in penitence and to receive his forgiveness and love, for there is more joy in heaven over one lost sheep that returns than over 99 who have no need of repentance (Luke 15:7).

The season of Advent is about both the first and the second comings of Christ. First, it is about his coming in humility, being born in a stable, living a human life, dying a brutal death and rising again. Second, it is about his coming in glory, his coming to judge the world, to sort the sheep from the goats. Advent is our God-given opportunity to prepare to meet Christ. Like Lent, it is a penitential season when the liturgical colour is purple. Yet, for many of us, Advent becomes so filled with busyness that there is little time to pray. Are we willing to make time to wait on God this Advent?

In a couple of weeks we shall look at John the Baptist, whose urgent call to repentance at Jesus' first coming is very similar to the challenge in today's passage, which anticipates his second coming. As we journey through Advent, let us examine ourselves and, by God's grace, root out and cast off those things that are dark. Let us put on the armour of light, praying that Christ will fill every part of our lives now, as we wait in anticipation for his coming to reign eternally over all lives in his kingdom of justice, peace and love.

The reward of longing, waiting and believing is beyond price!

Prayer: the Advent Collect

Almighty God, give us grace to cast away the works of darkness and to put on the armour of light, now in the time of this mortal life, in which your Son Jesus Christ came to us in great humility, that on the last day, when he shall come again in his glorious majesty to judge the living and the dead, we may rise to the life immortal; through him who is alive and reigns with you and the Holy Spirit, one God, now and for ever. Amen.[1]

Where is God for me?

Now the Lord said to Abram, 'Go from your country and your kindred and your father's house to the land that I will show you. I will make of you a great nation, and I will bless you, and make your name great, so that you will be a blessing. I will bless those who bless you, and the one who curses you I will curse; and in you all the families of the earth shall be blessed.'

So Abram went, as the Lord had told him; and Lot went with him. Abram was seventy-five years old when he departed from Haran. Abram took his wife Sarai and his brother's son Lot, and all the possessions that they had gathered, and the persons whom they had acquired in Haran; and they set forth to go to the land of Canaan. When they had come to the land of Canaan, Abram passed through the land to the place at Shechem, to the oak of Moreh. At that time the Canaanites were in the land. Then the Lord appeared to Abram, and said, 'To your offspring I will give this land.' So he built there an altar to the Lord, who had appeared to him.

GENESIS 12:1–7

At the beginning of our journey through Advent, we light the first Advent candle to symbolise the Old Testament patriarchs, of whom Abraham is chief. Abraham emerges, after the primeval history in the first eleven chapters of Genesis, as God's chosen vehicle to bless all the families of the earth. Humans had messed up big time, rebelling against God and falling out with each other. Today's passage, including God's promise to Abraham, marks the beginning of God's plan to redeem the world from its sin and corruption. People would be longing and waiting for two millennia for God to fulfil his promise. Then, through Jesus, the whole world would be blessed: 'For God so loved the world that he gave his only Son, so that everyone who believes in him may not perish but may have eternal life' (John 3:16). Nearly 2000 years before Christ came, however, Abraham 'believed the Lord; and the Lord reckoned it to him as righteousness' (Genesis 15:6).

Abraham is summoned from his own people to go to another country, an unknown land. I remember, when I finished my curacy, feeling that God was asking my wife and me to wait and see what we were to do next, rather than taking up another post immediately. A few weeks later an advertisement in *The Church Times* hit us both square in the face, and it seemed that God was calling us to go to Germany for a time. We set out on a snowy New Year's Day 2002, towing a small trailer with all the belongings we would need for the next seven months. On the evening of the following day we arrived in Heidelberg, where we were to serve the English Church as Chaplain and Reader.

For us, this was a significant step of faith and a great adventure, which has proved of lasting importance on our own journey of discipleship. We had to grapple with another language, adapt to a new currency and adjust to another culture, but we learnt so much, not least about ourselves.

We made many friends and I trust that, by God's grace, we had some impact on those whom we met and served.

Germany, as a European country, is not so very different from Britain, and many people today go to far more exotic parts of the world to serve God. However, in the ancient Near East nearly four millennia ago, how much more adventurous and perilous would have been Abraham's journey! He was called to journey into the unknown, simply taking on trust what God had promised. With his wife Sarah, nephew Lot and all their retinue and possessions, they would have formed a considerable caravan, and life was to prove hazardous and testing as Abraham sought to follow the divine command.

Germany is a modern democracy, but it has had a chequered history, particularly, of course, in the 20th century. My hero Dietrich Bonhoeffer, whom you will hear more about in subsequent pages, was teaching in the United States in July 1939 as war loomed, and had the opportunity to stay there. He paced the streets of New York asking himself the question, 'Where is God for me?' The answer for Bonhoeffer was, back in Germany with his own people. His inner turmoil vanished on the boat journey back, as he returned, an opponent of the Nazi régime, to face whatever might come.

As we set out on our journey of faith this Advent, I should like to challenge us to think about God's call on our own lives. Advent is a time of prayerful preparation to meet the Lord. We need, in line with yesterday's reading, to 'lay aside every weight and the sin that clings so closely' (Hebrews 12:1). Today's passage reminds us that we may even need to abandon our past life altogether. Certainly we need to focus on God and his will for us. Are we listening to him? Are we waiting on God, expectantly looking to him to teach us something new, lead us deeper into himself or take us in a new direction? Are we longing for God to act or are we afraid that he might actually do so, perhaps because we are just too settled in our comfortable ways? Might God even be calling us out of the life we have settled into, and asking something radically different of us? Where does God want me to be today, or tomorrow, or in five years' time? Are we prepared for the adventure that is life with God? Are we prepared to ask, with Bonhoeffer, 'Where is God for me?'

Abraham was 75 years old when he left Haran. God, for him, was in Canaan, where, we are told, he built an altar and the Lord appeared to him (v. 7). It is never too late to heed God's call.

For reflection and prayer

Ask yourself:

- *Where is God for me?*
- *Where is God for me in my work, my family and my community?*
- *Is God wanting me to journey in a new direction in my church involvement, in my relationship with him?*

Talk to God about your journey ahead and your adventure of life with him.

Waiting for the Lord's answer

Now Sarai, Abram's wife, bore him no children. She had an Egyptian slave-girl whose name was Hagar, and Sarai said to Abram, 'You see that the Lord has prevented me from bearing children; go in to my slave-girl; it may be that I shall obtain children by her.' And Abram listened to the voice of Sarai. So, after Abram had lived for ten years in the land of Canaan, Sarai, Abram's wife, took Hagar the Egyptian, her slave-girl, and gave her to her husband Abram as a wife. He went in to Hagar, and she conceived; and when she saw that she had conceived, she looked with contempt on her mistress. Then Sarai said to Abram, 'May the wrong done to me be on you! I gave my slave-girl to your embrace, and when she saw that she had conceived, she looked on me with contempt. May the Lord judge between you and me!' But Abram said to Sarai, 'Your slave-girl is in your power; do to her as you please.' Then Sarai dealt harshly with her, and she ran away from her.

GENESIS 16:1–6

One of the things that most appeals to me in the stories of the Old Testament is how God works through imperfect human beings. Abraham and Sarah are lauded as heroes of faith by the writer to the Hebrews (Hebrews 11:8–12), yet they exhibited only too human failings, as did the others whom we shall meet in the next few days. I find this a great encouragement. God can work through each one of us, despite our faults.

Abraham believes God's initial call and acts on it, but he fails subsequently in a number of ways. When he goes to Egypt to escape famine, he passes off Sarah as his sister (Genesis 12:12), and he does the same thing later on, in Gerar (20:1–2). In today's passage, Abraham listens to Sarah, who is barren, and is persuaded to father a child (named Ishmael) with her maid Hagar instead. Later still, Sarah laughs when three mysterious visitors arrive and the Lord repeats the promise that she will conceive (18:9–15). So the belief of Abraham and Sarah wavered, but God was working his purposes out all the same. As Paul explains in Galatians 4:21–31, there is an allegorical meaning to all this: Hagar represents the old covenant, the law given on Mount Sinai, and Ishmael is the child of slavery. Barren Sarah had to wait until she was very old to have her child, Isaac, but the wait was more than worth it. Isaac, the child God promised, corresponds to the new covenant, and we are heirs of this child of freedom.

We may long for God's answer to our prayers, for him to fulfil his promises, but do we have the patience to wait for him to do so? Do we really believe that he will answer or, like Abraham and Sarah, do we try to pre-empt God and do things in our own strength, in our own human way? Going against God's plan, being arrogant enough to think we know better, can only lead to trouble. A downward spiral can so easily follow, as it did for Sarah and Hagar (Genesis 16:4–6). Hagar, who was able to conceive, despised Sarah who couldn't. Sarah blamed Abraham for the outcome of the events she herself had engineered. Abraham simply let Sarah treat her maid as she pleased, which meant badly.

Later (21:9), we read that Sarah saw the young teenager Ishmael playing with her infant son Isaac. Did Sarah worry that Ishmael, being older, would be able to injure Isaac (as the Jewish historian Josephus suggests)?[2] Reflecting rabbinic interpretation, Paul tells us that Ishmael did indeed persecute Isaac (Galatians 4:29). So there was strife between the sons too, and the upshot was the expulsion of Hagar and Ishmael at Sarah's behest (Genesis 21:10–12). What a catalogue of broken relationships!

It is encouraging, however, that God can use our mistakes and our failures. Our generous God made a great nation of Ishmael too (16:10; 21:13). Twelve princes were born to him (25:16). God is faithful and keen to bless, even when we make a hash of things. We might cruelly reject a person out of envy, spite or fear; God never does.

When put to the severest test and commanded to sacrifice Isaac—the son of promise, the son of freedom—Abraham did not fail (22:1–14). This is a perplexing command as well as a horrifying one, since elsewhere in the Old Testament God's people are forbidden to practise child sacrifice: this was something that only their pagan neighbours did. In the event, God provided a substitute, a ram caught in a thicket.

This story surely strikes us, as Christians, as a foreshadowing of the sacrifice of Christ on the cross, when God himself did not withhold his only son (22:16) but gave him up for the salvation of the world. Even here at the beginning of our Advent journey, we are reminded of what it is all about, of where it is all heading: we await the coming of the Messiah, the Son of God, through whom 'all the families on earth shall be blessed'. Christ, when he is 'lifted up from the earth' (meaning lifted up on the cross) will 'draw all people' to himself (John 12:32).

There is much to ponder in today's reading. Do we try to pre-empt God and do things in our own strength rather than relying on him? When we get things wrong, do we make them worse by taking it out on others? While we long for God to work, do we have the patience to wait for him to answer our prayers and fulfil his promises? Augustine's mother Monica had to wait till her son was 32 before she saw her prayers answered and her son return to the faith in which she had nurtured him. Abraham was taken from his kindred aged 75 but was 100 by the time Isaac was born: Ishmael was already 14 by then. Could we wait and sustain our belief in God's promises for that long?

For reflection and prayer

Each day for the rest of this week, perhaps at the end of the day and in a quiet place, ask God for the gift of patience, in one of these ways:

- *For four or five minutes, repeat over and over Psalm 27:14: 'Wait for the Lord; be strong, and let your heart take courage; wait for the Lord!'*
- *Get hold of a recording (on CD or YouTube) of the Taizé chant 'Wait for the Lord, his day is near' and listen or sing along to it several times: 'Wait for the Lord, his day is near. Wait for the Lord, be strong, take heart.'*

Encountering the living God

The same night [Jacob] got up and took his two wives, his two maids, and his eleven children, and crossed the ford of the Jabbok. He took them and sent them across the stream, and likewise everything that he had. Jacob was left alone; and a man wrestled with him until daybreak. When the man saw that he did not prevail against Jacob, he struck him on the hip socket; and Jacob's hip was put out of joint as he wrestled with him. Then he said, 'Let me go, for the day is breaking.' But Jacob said, 'I will not let you go, unless you bless me.' So he said to him, 'What is your name?' And he said, 'Jacob.' Then the man said, 'You shall no longer be called Jacob, but Israel, for you have striven with God and with humans, and have prevailed.' Then Jacob asked him, 'Please tell me your name.' But he said, 'Why is it that you ask my name?' And there he blessed him. So Jacob called the place Peniel, saying, 'For I have seen God face to face, and yet my life is preserved.' The sun rose upon him as he passed Penuel, limping because of his hip. Therefore to this day the Israelites do not eat the thigh muscle that is on the hip socket, because he struck Jacob on the hip socket at the thigh muscle.

GENESIS 32:22–32

This deeply mysterious passage marks a turning point in the life of the patriarch Jacob. He wrestles with God and prevails, and he receives his new name, Israel. Likewise, Abraham (formerly Abram) had received a new name from God. It happened when God made his covenant of circumcision with Abram and sealed the promise that Abraham would be 'the ancestor of a multitude of nations' (Genesis 17:5), a promise that was later renewed to Jacob, Abraham's grandson (35:9–12).

The name of a person, in the ancient world, signified the person's character, and the name Jacob meant 'deceiver' or 'cheat'. Here again is a biblical example of how God uses flawed characters to work out his plan of salvation for the world. How reassuring that God might actually be able to use me!

Jacob was a cheat from his birth. He took hold of Esau's heel as they were being born, so from the start he was an attempted usurper (Genesis 25:26). Then he enticed Esau into selling his birthright for a bowl of lentil stew (vv. 29–34) and obtained his father Isaac's blessing by disguising himself as Esau (27:18–29). Jacob got his come-uppance years later when his father-in-law Laban cheated him of the wife he desired, but got his own back by cheating Laban out of his flocks. Yet this cheat was the man chosen to be the father of God's people, the Israelites.

We meet Jacob today on a journey. He was returning to the land of his birth, the land to which God had called his grandfather Abraham. He was also going to meet his brother Esau, and he was in great fear because of the history between them (32:7–8). In his wrestling match with the mysterious night-time visitor (a man who transpires to be God himself), Jacob would not let his opponent go until he received a blessing from him. At this point he was given his new name, Israel, meaning 'The one who strives with God'. Jacob had striven with God and humans—Esau and Laban—and prevailed.

The new name signified a new character for Jacob, and it signified the character of the nation that God would create through Jacob's descendants. The history of this nation was to be one of struggle with God and humans—a struggle in which they would ultimately prevail, because the Saviour of the world would be born from this line, in fulfilment of God's plan. In Jacob's immediate context, it meant that he could be confident in meeting the brother he had swindled. The next chapter brings a moving scene of reconciliation between the brothers, which is an important prelude to the final resolution of family conflict, as we shall see in the next two days.

It is still early in our own Advent journey, so let us ask how Jacob's experience is matched by our own. Are there damaged relationships that need to be repaired? Do we have the courage to go and mend fences with those we have wronged? Is our own character one of deceit, maybe even self-deceit, or is it one of wrestling with God and being blessed by him? If we are truly honest with ourselves, we shall recognise our character faults and the aspects of our lives that displease God. Do we long for God to change us, to give us a 'new name', to bless us? Let us pray for that, as we await the ultimate fulfilment of God's promises to Jacob in the coming of Christ.

Numinous experiences, mysterious encounters with the divine, are not confined to the characters of the Bible—far from it; they are remarkably widespread. They have been the subject of scientific study from about 1900 (by William James) until the present day. This line of research shows how difficult it is to deny the authenticity of religious experience, and the main point is that real authenticity is shown by the change in people's lives that so often results from an encounter with the living God.

Jacob wrestled with God and was marked for life, physically, having to live out his days with a limp. He was no longer the one in control of his life, no longer the strong man he had once been (Genesis 29:10). Our wrestling with God, our encounter with him, will leave its mark, as did Jacob's. It will weaken us in that we shall be brought down to size, but it will also make us stronger. We shall have to rely on God's strength, not on our own strength. We shall have to relinquish the control we had over our lives and give it up to God. Are we prepared for that?

For reflection and prayer

Why not have a time of self-examination in which to ponder the questions raised above? Then either read Psalm 51 or use the prayer below:

I desire, O gracious Lord, from this moment to renounce everything that may displease you, and resolve, with the help of your Holy Spirit, to resist all temptations, and to become completely yours; for in my own strength I can do nothing, but on you I depend entirely. For your name's sake, O Lord, and for the sake of your love and your promises, teach me whatever you would have me do, and then help me to do it. Teach me first what to resolve upon, and then enable me to perform my resolutions, that I may walk with you in the ways of holiness here, and rest with you in blessedness hereafter. Amen [3]

A family reunited

Then [Joseph] commanded the steward of his house, 'Fill the men's sacks with food, as much as they can carry, and put each man's money in the top of his sack. Put my cup, the silver cup, in the top of the sack of the youngest, with his money for the grain.' And he did as Joseph told him. As soon as the morning was light, the men were sent away with their donkeys. When they had gone only a short distance from the city, Joseph said to his steward, 'Go, follow after the men; and when you overtake them, say to them, "Why have you returned evil for good? Why have you stolen my silver cup? Is it not from this that my lord drinks? Does he not indeed use it for divination? You have done wrong in doing this."'

When he overtook them, he repeated these words to them. They said to him, 'Why does my lord speak such words as these? Far be it from your servants that they should do such a thing! Look, the money that we found at the top of our sacks, we brought back to you from the land of Canaan; why then would we steal silver or gold from your lord's house? Should it be found with any one of your servants, let him die; moreover, the rest of us will become my lord's slaves.' He said, 'Even so; in accordance with your words, let it be: he with whom it is found shall become my slave, but the rest of you shall go free.' Then each one quickly lowered his sack to the ground, and each opened his sack. He searched, beginning with the eldest and ending with the youngest; and the cup was found in Benjamin's sack. At this they tore their clothes. Then each one loaded his donkey, and they returned to the city.

Judah and his brothers came to Joseph's house while he was still there; and they fell to the ground before him. Joseph said to them, 'What deed is this that you have done? Do you not know that one such as I can practise divination?' And Judah said, 'What can we say to my lord? What can we speak? How can we clear ourselves? God has found out the guilt of your servants; here we are then, my lord's slaves, both we and also the one in whose possession the cup has been found.' But he said, 'Far be it from me that I should do so! Only the one in whose possession the cup was found shall be my slave; but as for you, go up in peace to your father.'

GENESIS 44:1–17

Our final encounter with the patriarchs involves Jacob's sons, the fathers of the twelve tribes of Israel. As I write, the Middle East, where the action of the book of Genesis takes place, is daily in the news. The reason we hear about it today is that it is a region of seemingly endless conflict. We hear a great deal about the conflict, but we never seem to hear about any work of reconciliation. Yet this work does happen, as I know from personal experience.

I had the great privilege of being ordained in Coventry Cathedral, a building packed with symbolism. On the very night it was bombed in 1940, the Provost, Richard Howard, stood in the ruins of his burned-out cathedral. He took charred beams from the roof, made a cross and a makeshift altar, and inscribed under it the words 'Father, forgive'. From that moment a work of reconciliation grew out of the ashes of the old cathedral.

The priest in charge of the International Ministry while I was in Coventry was Canon Andrew White. He is now Vicar of St George's, Baghdad, but at the time he was heavily involved in reconciliation in the Holy Land through the 'Alexandria Process'.

In 2003, my wife Shirley and I were in Berlin for the big church convention known as the Kirchentag. Along with a couple of thousand others, we attended an event at which Andrew was on the platform alongside three religious leaders, with whom he had been working closely in the Holy Land. They were Rabbi Michael Melchior, a member of the Knesset; Sheikh Talal el-Sider, a former Hamas terrorist and member of the Palestinian authority; and Michel Sabah, the Roman Catholic Patriarch of Jerusalem. Through Andrew's work, these three had been enabled to embrace each other as brothers, to share each other's pain and to agree on the need to share the land.

Rabbi Melchior gave us a brilliant overview of the book of Genesis. He said that the key to the book was the theme of brothers falling out, and he was right. Just think about it. The first murderer is Cain, who kills his brother Abel. Then there are Isaac and Ishmael, whom we considered a couple of days ago: their story has resonances today, as Jews and Arabs regard themselves as the respective descendants of these two. Then come Jacob and Esau, and finally Joseph and his brothers who sold him into slavery in Egypt.

The resolution, the rabbi explained, comes when the brothers are finally reconciled, and this happens when Judah takes responsibility for Benjamin. Today we have read how Joseph set a test for his brothers. He planted his silver cup in

Benjamin's sack, then accused him of theft and commanded that he be held as a slave while the others were allowed to return to their father. In the verses following today's extract, Judah volunteers to stay behind as Joseph's slave instead (44:18–34). This represents a marked change of character on the part of Judah. Benjamin was Joseph's younger brother and the others were really half-brothers, so their treatment of Benjamin is crucial. Indeed, the story is shot through with the guilt now felt by the brothers over their former treatment of Joseph. Tomorrow we shall see how the story is completed and how, after many years, harmony is restored, the family is reunited and all are brought together to live with Joseph in security in Egypt.

What lessons does this story of conflict resolution hold for us today? Well, if we are reconciled to God like Joseph, as I trust we are, then we too can become instruments of reconciliation. Our own families, our workplaces, even our churches, sad to say, can be places of rivalry and conflict. In a small way, can we be peacemakers and reconcilers rather than antagonists? Some readers may have a bigger role to play on a bigger stage, for none of us knows what God may seek to do through us in the future. Andrew White was vicar of an ordinary parish in South London before being thrust into the world of international diplomacy and peacemaking on the world stage.

Reconciliation and peacemaking are always important, and it is especially fitting to dwell on them in Advent as we long for the completion of the process of reconciliation in Christ. Let us reflect on the truth that 'in Christ God was reconciling the world to himself, not counting their trespasses against them, and entrusting the message of reconciliation to us' (2 Corinthians 5:19).

For prayer

Either listen to a recording of the song 'Make me a channel of your peace' or use this form of the prayer attributed to St Francis:

Lord, make me an instrument of your peace.
Where there is hatred, let me sow love,
Where there is injury, pardon,
Where there is doubt, faith,
Where there is despair, hope,
Where there is darkness, light,
Where there is sadness, joy.

O Divine Master, grant that I may not so much seek
to be consoled as to console,
not so much to be understood as to understand,
not so much to be loved as to love,
for it is in giving that we receive,
it is in pardoning that we are pardoned,
it is in dying that we are born again to eternal life.

6 DECEMBER

God brings good out of evil

Then Joseph said to his brothers, 'Come closer to me.' And they came closer. He said, 'I am your brother Joseph, whom you sold into Egypt. And now do not be distressed, or angry with yourselves, because you sold me here; for God sent me before you to preserve life. For the famine has been in the land these two years; and there are five more years in which there will be neither ploughing nor harvest. God sent me before you to preserve for you a remnant on earth, and to keep alive for you many survivors. So it was not you who sent me here, but God; he has made me a father to Pharaoh, and lord of all his house and ruler over all the land of Egypt. Hurry and go up to my father and say to him, "Thus says your son Joseph, God has made me lord of all Egypt; come down to me, do not delay. You shall settle in the land of Goshen, and you shall be near me, you and your children and your children's children, as well as your flocks, your herds, and all that you have. I will provide for you there—since there are five more years of famine to come—so that you and your household, and all that you have, will not come to poverty." And now your eyes and the eyes of my brother Benjamin see that it is my own mouth that speaks to you. You must tell my father how greatly I am honoured in Egypt, and all that you have seen. Hurry and bring my father down here.' Then he fell upon his brother Benjamin's neck and wept, while Benjamin wept upon his neck. And he kissed all his brothers and wept upon them; and after that his brothers talked with him.

GENESIS 45:4–15

The story of Joseph and his brothers, besides being immensely moving at the human level, presents us with an even more important lesson than the one concerning a single family's reconciliation. It is vital to grasp what God is doing in the story. Three times in verses 5–8 the message is hammered home that God is the one who sent Joseph to Egypt, because God had a greater plan.

Some of the questions we wrestle with in the science–religion dialogue are, 'How does God act in the world? How does he bring about his purposes in a world described by scientific laws? And if God has given humans genuine free will, how can we understand that in such a universe?' In answer, we talk about how our understanding of the universe is no longer as the clockwork mechanism that Newton and Laplace suggested. Rather, it is a place of genuine becoming, of new and surprising emergent phenomena, which are unpredictable from the laws of nature we have discovered. These insights may help us a little in understanding how both God and humans might act, given that the world is not deterministic and predictable after all—but the mystery remains.

Scripture is quite clear in seeing God in ultimate control, bringing about his purposes, *and* human beings making choices. Humans can freely choose between right and wrong. So Joseph's brothers intended evil but God intended good, and, through the brothers' own actions, he brought rescue many years later. Indeed, it was through this wayward and dysfunctional patriarchal family that God always intended to bring about reconciliation, not just for these brothers but for the whole world. As we have seen, Jacob's new name, Israel, means 'the one who struggles with God', and so it is with his family, too.

The promise to Jacob's grandfather Abraham, that all the nations of the world would be blessed through his family, was ultimately fulfilled in Christ. That ultimate fulfilment was kept on track throughout the shifting fortunes, jealousies, conflicts and rebellion of the characters in our story. They were rescued from death by famine because Joseph, whom his brothers had sold into slavery, had risen to pre-eminence in Egypt. Peter made a similar point over 1500 years later when he addressed the crowds at Pentecost, saying, 'This man, handed over to you according to the definite plan and foreknowledge of God, you crucified and killed by the hands of those outside the law' (Acts 2:23). It was a free decision by sinful human beings to put Jesus to death, but that was the culmination of God's plan to save the world.

Joseph's story is not an isolated instance of God's rescue. God's deliverance is a theme running throughout scripture and is especially prominent in Genesis. Noah was rescued from the flood; Abraham was taken from his family; Lot was rescued from Sodom; and here, as Joseph said, 'God sent me before you to preserve for you a remnant on earth' (Genesis 45:7). The word 'remnant' is often a word of hope in the Old Testament, and so Joseph interprets it here. In all the confused events of the past, God has been working to save his people; and Joseph, realising that human passions can so easily be aroused, tells the brothers that they are not to be distressed, warning them as they depart, 'Do not quarrel along the way' (v. 24).

When the brothers returned to their father Jacob, he was sceptical. However, when they told him all the words of Joseph and he saw the loaded wagons, he believed. Jacob's decision to go to Egypt is confirmed in Genesis 46:3 when, in a vision, God gives him a renewed promise that he will indeed become a great nation in Egypt.

An obvious lesson is that, whatever the appearances, and no matter how deep a mire we get ourselves into, God is in control. God has higher plans; indeed, his ultimate plan is to save us as he saved Israel of old, and he can do that despite our mistakes and our sins. As we have seen before, maybe an even harder lesson is to be patient and to wait for God's saving action when we are in a mess, depressed or at rock bottom. The Joseph saga took 22 years to reach its consummation. Remaining patient for so long must seem like waiting for an eternity, but it can be unimaginably rewarding.

The philosopher John Lucas gives an encouraging analogy for God's providential action, using the picture of rugmaking in a Persian family. The children weave from one end and the father from the opposite end of the rug. The father takes into account whatever mistakes his children make, and skilfully works the whole into a beautiful pattern. That is what God does with our lives. Despite the mistakes we make and the bad things others do to us, God is working towards something beautiful—ultimately, to life in perfect union with him. If we can accept that, then I think we have the prospect of deeply fulfilled lives, lived in the security and knowledge that we are part of God's deepest purposes.

For reflection

Take a few minutes to reflect on the way God has brought you to where you are today, maybe from where you were five or ten years ago. Can you think back to a mistake you have made in life? Can you see now how God has turned it to good? If not, can you trust him to bring about his plans for the future?

Foretelling God's plan

With the lighting of the second Advent candle, we move on in time and join the Old Testament prophets, who look forward to a day when God's justice will become reality. Their horizon seems to stretch from their immediate context to a future when God will act in a radically new way. A son is to be born, who will usher in endless peace, justice and righteousness. Yet God's servant will suffer, not for his own sins but for the sins of others, and God will depose the shepherds of his flock and take charge himself. God's mercy will be extended to all who repent.

The Day of the Lord

Alas for you who desire the day of the Lord!
Why do you want the day of the Lord?
It is darkness, not light;
as if someone fled from a lion,
  and was met by a bear;
or went into the house and rested a hand against the wall,
and was bitten by a snake.
Is not the day of the Lord darkness, not light,
and gloom with no brightness in it?
I hate, I despise your festivals,
and I take no delight in your solemn assemblies.
Even though you offer me your burnt-offerings
  and grain-offerings,
I will not accept them;
and the offerings of well-being of your fatted animals
I will not look upon.
Take away from me the noise of your songs;
I will not listen to the melody of your harps.
But let justice roll down like waters,
and righteousness like an ever-flowing stream.

AMOS 5:18–24

Today we start to focus on another major theme of Advent—
the prophets—and we begin with the great pre-exilic critic

of social injustice, Amos. Amos was a shepherd from Tekoa, a village in Judah about six miles south of Bethlehem. He prophesied in the eighth century BC during the reigns of King Uzziah of Judah and King Jeroboam II of Israel, and is the first of the 'classical' prophets (meaning those whose oracles we have as a book). During a time when many felt at ease, he spoke a word of judgement.

The Israelites expected the 'day of the Lord' to be the day when God would come and judge all their enemies, so it was something they looked forward to. They had to realise, though, that it would be very uncomfortable for them too. Amos begins with oracles against the surrounding nations (1:3—2:3), which might have lulled Israel into a sense of security and superiority, but then, from 2:4 onward, comes a devastating criticism of the people of God.

The 'day of the Lord' will be bad for Israel because they have violated their covenant with God. They have kept up the appearance of devotion, but this means nothing to God because reality is measured by how they have treated the poor and vulnerable. There is human trafficking (2:6), oppression of the poor, sexual immorality (2:7), and the taking of bribes (5:12)—a dreadful catalogue of wrongdoing. What God really asks is that 'justice roll down like waters, and righteousness like an ever-flowing stream' (5:24). The result of violating the true meaning of the covenant will be destruction, and the prophet warns of it in no uncertain terms.

Amos's message had a direct relevance to the people of the day as, first, the northern kingdom of Israel and then, more than a century later, the southern kingdom of Judah were taken into captivity. There is a sense in which there is, or seems to be, an inevitable sequence of cause and effect in the world, and evil brings retribution on to itself. It is as if God has built this sequence of cause and effect into human affairs, just as he has built scientific laws into the natural world. Corrupt and oppressive societies tend to implode: witness the collapse of communism in the Eastern bloc. If countries are aggressive to their neighbours, they come to naught in the end. Nevertheless, oppressive regimes can wreak havoc while they have power, and scripture is also realistic in raising the question, 'Why does the way of the guilty prosper?' (Jeremiah 12:1). Ultimately, however, all shall be accountable to God and have to give an answer for their conduct.

Amos's prophecy also has a direct relevance to Advent as we prepare to meet the judge of the world, Jesus, God's incarnate Son. This is indeed a recurring Advent theme and will be brought out even more strongly when we meet John the Baptist, the last of the prophets. We need to examine our own lives. Is our devotion to God genuine or merely an outward show? Can it be measured by our love for both God and neighbour? Is there anybody worse off than ourselves whom we are exploiting or oppressing—say, as an employer? More subtly, are we indirectly exploiting others through our purchase of goods made in places where the health and safety of workers are ignored? In that case, we need to hold the Western companies engaged in such practices to account. Then we should ask ourselves whether our sexual conduct is above reproach. Are we honest in affairs of money? Is our business practice above board? Do we use the gifts we have been given by God—including our monetary wealth—for his service and to help those who are poor and suffering, or for our own selfish ends?

There is much to consider as we await 'the day of the Lord'. Will it be, for us, a day of condemnation or a joyful day of meeting the Lord whom we know now as our loving and forgiving Saviour? If the latter, then it is by the sheer grace of God, and not because of our merits. Whatever our faults and sins, they can be forgiven and we can be changed.

There is good news, even at the end of Amos's grim tirade against the multifarious sins of the nations, Israel and Judah included. Although we humans are unfaithful, God remains faithful to his promises. Despite all that has gone before, God says, 'I will restore the fortunes of my people Israel, and they shall rebuild the ruined cities and inhabit them; they shall plant vineyards and drink their wine, and they shall make gardens and eat their fruit. I will plant them upon their land, and they shall never again be plucked up out of the land that I have given them' (Amos 9:14–15).

For reflection

You might like to look at 2 Timothy 2:13 and ask yourself these questions (which we considered above):

- *Is my devotion to God genuine or merely an outward show?*
- *Is there anybody worse off than me, whom I am exploiting or oppressing—say, as an employer?*
- *Am I indirectly exploiting others through my purchase of goods made in places where the health and safety of workers are ignored?*
- *Is my sexual conduct above reproach?*
- *Am I honest in affairs of money?*
- *Is my business practice above board?*
- *Do I use the gifts I have been given by God—including my monetary wealth—for his service and to help those who are poor and suffering, or for my own selfish ends?*

Prophesying hope

The people who walked in darkness
have seen a great light;
those who lived in a land of deep darkness—
on them light has shined.
You have multiplied the nation,
you have increased its joy;
they rejoice before you
as with joy at the harvest,
as people exult when dividing plunder.
For the yoke of their burden,
and the bar across their shoulders,
the rod of their oppressor,
you have broken as on the day of Midian.
For all the boots of the tramping warriors
and all the garments rolled in blood
shall be burned as fuel for the fire.
For a child has been born for us,
a son given to us;
authority rests upon his shoulders;
and he is named
Wonderful Counsellor, Mighty God,
Everlasting Father, Prince of Peace.
His authority shall grow continually,
and there shall be endless peace

for the throne of David and his kingdom.
He will establish and uphold it
with justice and with righteousness
from this time onwards and for evermore.
The zeal of the Lord of hosts will do this.

ISAIAH 9:2–7

Isaiah was prophesying in Jerusalem, the capital of Judah, shortly after Amos was doing the same at Bethel in the northern kingdom. His oracles have some features in common with those of Amos, including criticism of worship and judgement against the nations—again, not just the enemies of God's people but Israel and Judah as well. There is also a strong message of hope, and this is brought out especially in the messianic oracles, such as the one we have read today.

The prophet speaks of a child to be born who will be king and will sit on the throne of David. Through this future ruler, the nation will be blessed. He will bring light to those dwelling in darkness; oppression and violence will be banished, and peace, justice and righteousness will be established for ever.

As with many prophecies, there may be a double reference. Perhaps the immediate fulfilment was the birth of King Hezekiah, who 'did what was right in the sight of the Lord' (2 Kings 18:3). Indeed, we are told that he was a king such as there had never been before or since (v. 5). He purified the worship and was victorious in battle. He refused to serve the Assyrians, and God gave Judah a remarkable deliverance during his reign, when Sennacherib's army besieged Jerusalem (19:35–37).

While this might be the immediate meaning of the text, its fulfilment in Hezekiah was, at best, partial. His government did come to an end, unlike the rule of the king in the prophecy, even though God gave Hezekiah 15 more years of life in response to his prayer (Isaiah 38:1–6). No king in David's line ruled 'for evermore' (Isaiah 9:7)—that is, no king until Jesus.

So there is a far future aspect to this prophecy, too. Jesus alone is the king who will bring peace, justice and righteousness for evermore. No king apart from Jesus could be called 'Wonderful Counsellor, Prince of Peace', and, in particular, no other king could embody the divine epithets 'Mighty God' and 'Everlasting Father'. Jesus, God incarnate, is indeed the king of David's line who fulfils this remarkable prophecy.

By the time Jesus came, Israel's monarchy had been over for many centuries. The end came when Judah was taken into exile (587BC). There were hopes for its restoration under Zerubbabel, on the return from exile, but these hopes came to nothing. Neither the Hasmoneans, who won a degree of autonomy for the Jews in the second century BC, nor Herod the Great and his successors, who were puppet regents, were really kings of the Davidic line.

Astonishingly, the true Davidic King-Messiah, the son given to us, was a child born not in a royal palace in Jerusalem but in a cattle shed in Bethlehem. Jesus upset all the expectations for a ruler by being born in such humility rather than in the luxury of a palace. Moreover, he brought about his kingdom of peace, justice and righteousness in an unexpected way. He did not do so by waging war or assembling an army to drive out the Romans, Israel's latest conquerors. Instead, his kingdom was established by his living a perfect life of sacrificial service, dying on a cross and rising again.

By dying and rising again, Jesus brings about the peace that is the foundation for all peace—namely, peace between God and human beings, who, by their sinfulness, have alienated themselves from God. From this peace, the peace between individuals and between nations will follow.

The resurrection of Jesus anticipates the final fulfilment of the messianic prophecies of Isaiah, perhaps especially in Isaiah 11, where the prophecy is even more clearly futuristic than in chapter 9. The prophecy that 'the wolf shall live with the lamb [and] the leopard shall lie down with the kid' (11:6) is referring to an ideal future state, not physically realisable with the laws of nature as they currently operate. Science tells us that wolves' jaws, teeth and digestive systems are adapted very precisely to devour lambs, so something dramatic has to happen for that to change.

In the light of Christ we can see, perhaps even more clearly than Isaiah himself could see, that future state when 'they will not hurt or destroy on all my holy mountain; for the earth will be full of the knowledge of the Lord as the waters cover the sea' (11:9). Isaiah knew the character of God—his faithfulness and justice, his love, and his longing that people would live by his laws, which were decreed for their benefit. Isaiah trusted God that he would one day bring about a kingdom of peace and justice. It just had to happen, given the character of God and his power to do it.

In his oracles of future hope, Isaiah gives us hints as to how God might accomplish his purposes—but how surprising that it should come about in the way it actually did, in Christ! Our God is indeed a 'God of surprises'. We are in the privileged position of seeing how it all makes sense in a more wonderful way than even the Old Testament prophets could have imagined. Jesus brings about a kingdom of love, peace, joy and righteousness, which will indeed go on 'for evermore'. Alleluia!

For reflection

Handel's Messiah *is one of the most inspired musical compositions of all time, with the libretto taken entirely from scripture. Listen to the chorus 'For unto us a child is born' (*Messiah *Part 1, No. 12), meditating on the amazing way in which God's gift of his own Son was foretold more than seven centuries ahead of time.*

Changed from the inside

The days are surely coming, says the Lord, when I will make a new covenant with the house of Israel and the house of Judah. It will not be like the covenant that I made with their ancestors when I took them by the hand to bring them out of the land of Egypt—a covenant that they broke, though I was their husband, says the Lord. But this is the covenant that I will make with the house of Israel after those days, says the Lord: I will put my law within them, and I will write it on their hearts; and I will be their God, and they shall be my people. No longer shall they teach one another, or say to each other, 'Know the Lord', for they shall all know me, from the least of them to the greatest, says the Lord; for I will forgive their iniquity, and remember their sin no more.

JEREMIAH 31:31–34

Jeremiah prophesied from the reign of the reforming King Josiah (d. 609BC), through the first defeat and captivity of Judah by Nebuchadnezzar in 597BC, until the final fall of Jerusalem under Zedekiah in 587BC. This was the point at which the people were taken into captivity in Babylon, although Jeremiah was taken by a group of fugitives to Egypt.

Jeremiah's message is uncompromising. The people of

Judah have sinned against God by breaking his covenant. If they repent, they can stay in the land, worshipping in the Jerusalem temple, but, if not, they will be taken into exile in Babylon. They were called to repent and they were told not to resist Nebuchadnezzar, because that would be futile—an unpopular message if ever there was one.

Despite their rebellion, the people of Judah are still God's people, and he loves—indeed, yearns—for them: 'Is Ephraim my dear son? Is he the child I delight in? As often as I speak against him, I still remember him. Therefore I am deeply moved for him; I will surely have mercy on him, says the Lord' (Jeremiah 31:20).

What is the solution to this intractable problem? The history of God's people is, sadly, one of rebellion, but God's love is unconditional; he is faithful to his promises even if his people are not. There are consequences to sin: when we sin, it can harm us, just as the Israelites' rebellions harmed them. Mercifully, God had a wonderful revolutionary method for dealing with the problem. He promised Jeremiah that one day he would make a new covenant. The old covenant that God made with his people was written on tablets of stone and given to Moses at Mount Sinai. The new covenant would be quite different, for it would be within them and written on their hearts. This makes all the difference. Now, God's people can know him directly, not second-hand by being told about him. The prophet Ezekiel goes even further:

A new heart I will give you, and a new spirit I will put within you; and I will remove from your body the heart of stone and give you a heart of flesh. I will put my spirit within you, and make you follow my statutes and be careful to observe my ordinances. (Ezekiel 36:26–27)

What all this means is that we shall be changed from the inside. We shall be enabled to live God's way because his Spirit operates within us. Our hearts will no longer (metaphorically) be made of stone—hard and resistant to God's will. They will be made of flesh—soft, responsive and able to be moulded by God to think his thoughts and follow his will.

It is hard not to see the direct confirmation of this prophecy in what Jesus achieved 600 years later. Jeremiah was surely one of those 'many prophets and righteous people' who 'longed to see what you see, but did not see it, and to hear what you hear, but did not hear it' (Matthew 13:17). In John's Gospel we read how Jesus had to 'go away' (that is, die) so that 'the Advocate' (helper or counsellor) would come (John 16:7). What will the Advocate, the Holy Spirit, do but to fulfil Jeremiah's and Ezekiel's prophecies? 'When the Spirit of truth comes, he will guide you into all the truth; for he will not speak on his own, but will speak whatever he hears, and he will declare to you the things that are to come' (v. 13).

We see this fulfilment on the day of Pentecost, when the Spirit is given to the disciples and to all believers thereafter (Acts 2:33). As Paul puts it, we have been transferred into a new realm. We are no longer 'in the flesh', in our sins, but 'in the Spirit', in Christ, under new management: 'But if Christ is in you, though the body is dead because of sin, the Spirit is life because of righteousness. If the Spirit of him who raised Jesus from the dead dwells in you, he who raised Christ from the dead will give life to your mortal bodies also through his Spirit that dwells in you' (Romans 8:10–11).

What amazing riches we have in Christ! It is not just that he died for us and rose again—as if that weren't far more than enough—but he also changes us from the inside through the Spirit so that we can be like him. How can we possibly thank him enough?

For prayer

Use this hymn as a prayer:

Breathe on me, Breath of God,
Fill me with life anew,
That I may love what thou dost love,
And do what thou wouldst do.

Breathe on me, Breath of God,
Until my heart is pure;
Until with thee I will one will,
To do and to endure.

Breathe on me, Breath of God,
Till I am wholly thine;
Until this earthly part of me
Glows with thy fire divine.

Breathe on me, Breath of God:
So shall I never die,
But live with thee the perfect life
Of thine eternity.

E. HATCH

The Suffering Servant

Who has believed what we have heard?
And to whom has the arm of the Lord been revealed?
For he grew up before him like a young plant,
and like a root out of dry ground;
he had no form or majesty that we should look at him
nothing in his appearance that we should desire him.
He was despised and rejected by others;
a man of suffering and acquainted with infirmity;
and as one from whom others hide their faces
he was despised, and we held him of no account.
Surely he has borne our infirmities
and carried our diseases;
yet we accounted him stricken,
struck down by God, and afflicted.
But he was wounded for our transgressions,
crushed for our iniquities;
upon him was the punishment that made us whole,
and by his bruises we are healed.
All we like sheep have gone astray;
we have all turned to our own way,
and the Lord has laid on him
the iniquity of us all.

He was oppressed, and he was afflicted,
yet he did not open his mouth
like a lamb that is led to the slaughter,
and like a sheep that before its shearers is silent,
so he did not open his mouth.
By a perversion of justice he was taken away.
Who could have imagined his future?
For he was cut off from the land of the living,
stricken for the transgression of my people.
They made his grave with the wicked
and his tomb with the rich,
although he had done no violence,
and there was no deceit in his mouth.

ISAIAH 53:1–9

This marvellous and evocative passage from Isaiah is perhaps the prophecy *par excellence* of the suffering Messiah.

Scholars consider the middle part of the book of Isaiah to stem from the period of the Babylonian exile. King Nebuchadnezzar has invaded Judah, destroyed the temple, deposed the king and carted off the people—apart from a few lowly vine-dressers—into exile (2 Kings 25:12). Here the prophet (generally known as Deutero- or Second Isaiah) brings them encouragement.

Within the prophet's set of oracles are four 'servant songs', of which this is the last. The identity of the suffering servant is a matter of debate. Is it the prophet himself who is writing the songs, is it the people of Israel as a whole, or is it another mysterious individual? Whatever the writer himself understood by his inspired utterances, it is truly remarkable that they should be fulfilled in so detailed a way by Jesus.

Let's look at the passage in a bit more depth. First, it would seem that the narrator and his associates have heard something about the servant but have had difficulty in making others believe it. The servant himself has a hard time right from his upbringing. He is nothing to look at; his background is unpromising (a 'root out of dry ground'); he is despised and rejected; he is 'a man of suffering' and he is 'acquainted with infirmity'.

This is already very sombre, but the astonishing thing is that he suffers all this not on his own account but for the sake of others. He has borne 'our' infirmities and carried 'our' diseases. It was natural for the readers in Isaiah's culture to assume that the servant had been 'struck down by God' for his own sins. That was what Job's so-called comforters told him (wrongly in that case, too: see Job 2:3). The revolutionary thing about today's passage—the thing that is so hard to believe—is that he was wounded for our transgressions and crushed for our iniquities, and the end result of his actions is that we are made whole; we are healed by his bruises. All of us are sinful; we are all sheep who have gone astray. The evil we have done has been laid on the innocent suffering servant.

Doesn't so much of the message of this passage and the other servant songs (Isaiah 42:1–7; 49:1–7; 50:4–9), resonate with what the New Testament tells us about Jesus? He gave his back to those who struck him (50:6) when he was scourged; he was struck down by God when he suffered his agonising death on the cross. It looked as if he was being punished for his own sins, since 'cursed is everyone who hangs on a tree' (Galatians 3:13, echoing Deuteronomy 21:23). Jesus was innocent and sinless himself, yet he did all that—even becoming a curse—for us (2 Corinthians 5:21). As he himself said, he gave his life as a 'ransom for many' (Matthew 20:28), and, as Paul puts it, 'since all have sinned and fall short of the glory of God, they are now justified by his grace as a gift, through the redemption that is in Christ Jesus, whom God put forward as a sacrifice of atonement by his blood, effective through faith' (Romans 3:23–25). The Greek word for 'sacrifice of atonement' is a translation of the Hebrew for 'mercy seat', which covered the ark of the covenant and from where God dispensed mercy and wiped away the people's sins.

When Jesus stood before Pilate, 'he gave him no answer' (Matthew 27:14). A human judge presumed to judge the one who would judge the world, and condemned him to death. Jesus was crucified with criminals, but a rich man, Joseph of Arimathea, provided the grave. In the subsequent verses of Isaiah 53, we see that the servant is vindicated. Although he has suffered death, 'out of his anguish he shall see light' (v. 11).

In science, the closest analogy to prophecy is the prediction of phenomena that we should be able to observe in the laboratory or with our telescopes on the basis of our theory. The Higgs boson was predicted to exist by physicists in 1964 but was observed at the Large Hadron Collider only in 2012. This is quite a long gap between prediction and discovery for science but pales beside the truly remarkable prophecy of Deutero-Isaiah, made some 540 years before Jesus was born. Prophecy is a much less precise concept than prediction in science; nevertheless, it can count as evidence for the truth of Christian claims, just as prediction does for scientific theories.

Many people today, even Christians, find Deutero-Isaiah's message very hard to believe. Can it be fair and just for another person to suffer for my sin? Yet when we consider that Jesus is the incarnate Word—God from God, light from light, true God from true God—I believe it does make sense. It is not some other human person being unjustly punished by God; it is the incarnate Logos freely offering himself, freely taking upon himself the weight of human sin and making that offering available for our forgiveness so that we may be 'made righteous' (v. 11). After the longing and waiting of more than half a millennium for the prophecy to be fulfilled, and 2000 years after that until our own time, can we believe it?

For reflection

Reflect on this song, either by listening to a recording of it or by reading it slowly:

Broken for me, broken for you,
the body of Jesus broken for us.

He offered his body, he poured out his soul;
Jesus was broken that we might be whole.
Broken for me, broken for you,
the body of Jesus broken for us.

Come to my table and with me dine;
eat of my bread and drink of my wine.
Broken for me, broken for you,
the body of Jesus broken for us.

This is my body given for you;
eat it, remembr'ing I died for you.
Broken for me, broken for you,
the body of Jesus broken for us.

This is my blood I shed for you,
for your forgiveness, making you new.
Broken for me, broken for you,
the body of Jesus broken for us.

JANET LUNT, COPYRIGHT © 1978, SOVEREIGN MUSIC UK

Shepherding God's flock

The word of the Lord came to me: Mortal, prophesy against the shepherds of Israel: prophesy, and say to them—to the shepherds: Thus says the Lord God: Ah, you shepherds of Israel who have been feeding yourselves! Should not shepherds feed the sheep? You eat the fat, you clothe yourselves with the wool, you slaughter the fatlings; but you do not feed the sheep. You have not strengthened the weak, you have not healed the sick, you have not bound up the injured, you have not brought back the strayed, you have not sought the lost, but with force and harshness you have ruled them. So they were scattered, because there was no shepherd; and scattered, they became food for all the wild animals. My sheep were scattered, they wandered over all the mountains and on every high hill; my sheep were scattered over all the face of the earth, with no one to search or seek for them.

Therefore, you shepherds, hear the word of the Lord: As I live, says the Lord God, because my sheep have become a prey, and my sheep have become food for all the wild animals, since there was no shepherd; and because my shepherds have not searched for my sheep, but the shepherds have fed themselves, and have not fed my sheep; therefore, you shepherds, hear the word of the Lord: Thus says the Lord God, I am against the shepherds; and I will demand my sheep at their hand, and put a stop to their feeding the sheep; no longer shall the shepherds feed themselves. I will rescue my sheep from their mouths, so that they may not be food for them.

For thus says the Lord God: I myself will search for my sheep, and will seek them out. As shepherds seek out their flocks when they are among their scattered sheep, so I will seek out my sheep. I will rescue them from all the places to which they have been scattered on a day of clouds and thick darkness. I will bring them out from the peoples and gather them from the countries, and will bring them into their own land; and I will feed them on the mountains of Israel, by the watercourses, and in all the inhabited parts of the land. I will feed them with good pasture, and the mountain heights of Israel shall be their pasture; there they shall lie down in good grazing land, and they shall feed on rich pasture on the mountains of Israel. I myself will be the shepherd of my sheep, and I will make them lie down, says the Lord God. I will seek the lost, and I will bring back the strayed, and I will bind up the injured, and I will strengthen the weak, but the fat and the strong I will destroy. I will feed them with justice.

EZEKIEL 34:1–16

Ezekiel, like Deutero-Isaiah, is a prophet of the exile. He was taken with the captives to Babylon. The Jews had thought that God dwelt in the temple at Jerusalem, but Ezekiel found that God was with them in captivity. He had the most amazing visions and acted out parables in a highly eccentric manner. Authentic holiness can be hard to cope with, as we see from the lives of other saints down the ages.

In today's passage, the prophet is scathingly critical of the shepherds of Israel, the rulers who should have been looking after God's people. They have simply not been doing their job. The sheep have been neglected, the weak not strengthened, the sick not healed, and the strayed not brought back. Instead of looking after the sheep, the shepherds have fed themselves. It is a lesson for all of us, lay or ordained, who have pastoral responsibilities in our parishes, whether for adults who need our support or for children. Our priority is the well-being of the sheep, not of ourselves. A significant theme in Ezekiel is the awesome responsibility that the Lord's ministers carry (Ezekiel 3:18–19).

God's judgement on erring leaders is severe. He will rescue his sheep, and the false shepherds will no longer be allowed to feed themselves. The shepherds will be removed and God himself will take over as shepherd. God will bind up the injured and strengthen the weak. He will search out and bring back those who have strayed and feed them on rich pasture.

Those who heard Ezekiel's prophecy must have longed for its fulfilment. Its partial fulfilment took place when God brought back his people from captivity in Babylon under Cyrus the Great. Then they could once again feed 'on rich pasture on the mountains of Israel'—although the northern kingdom was never restored. Yet how wonderfully the prophecy was fulfilled by Jesus in the New Testament! His situation was remarkably like that in Ezekiel's time. As we shall explore in a few days' time, the Jews regarded themselves as being still in exile in Jesus' day, since their land was occupied by the Romans, and they were expecting God to liberate them finally and completely. But the shepherds at that time too—the priests and Levites who administered the temple, and the Pharisees who were 'holier than thou'—were not fulfilling their God-given roles of caring for the flock.

Jesus enters this situation as the 'good shepherd' (John 10:14). He tells how a real shepherd would search for one sheep out of a hundred, even if all the others had not strayed (Luke 15:3–7): 'There will be more joy in heaven over one sinner who repents than over ninty-nine righteous people who need no repentance.' The good shepherd exhibits qualities in direct contrast to those of the neglectful and selfish shepherds. As the 'gate for the sheep' (John 10:7), he saves those who enter the sheepfold, guarding them against thieves who come to steal and kill and destroy. Jesus took this imagery directly from his surroundings. A sheepfold on a hillside had a gap in which the shepherd lay, risking his life against ravening wolves. Indeed, Jesus tells us that the good shepherd lays down his life for the sheep (v. 15), in contrast to the hired hand who runs for his life when the wolf comes.

Just as the sheep of Ezekiel's day were scattered and needed to be brought back to their land, so too the good shepherd has other sheep 'that do not belong to this fold' whom he must 'bring also', so that 'there will be one flock, one shepherd' (v. 16). Jesus brings together, into his kingdom of love, both Jew and Gentile. Indeed, he unites people of every nationality and language. His Church is the one community on earth in which 'there is no longer Jew or Greek, there is no longer slave or free, there is no longer male and female; for all of you are one in Christ Jesus' (Galatians 3:28).

Ezekiel tells us that God will become the shepherd of his flock, deposing the shepherds who neglect the sheep. Amazingly, God did indeed become the shepherd in the person of his incarnate Son, Jesus, and, unlike the hired hand, he gave up his life to save the sheep. But the great truth is that this salvific act was not the end, because the shepherd, like Deutero-Isaiah's suffering servant, was vindicated: 'I lay down my life in order to take it up again. No one takes it from me, but I lay it down of my own accord. I have power to lay it down, and I have power to take it up again. I have received this command from my Father' (John 10: 17–18). How wonderful to be in the care of the good shepherd, the incarnate Son of God, who takes us into his everlasting kingdom of love!

For reflection

Use your imagination to picture the first-century shepherd lying across the gap in the sheepfold. Repeat Jesus' words slowly: 'I am the gate. Whoever enters by me will be saved, and will come in and go out and find pasture… I am the good shepherd… I lay down my life for the sheep' (John 10:9, 14–15). Thank Jesus that he laid down his life for the sheep.

12 DECEMBER

The reluctant prophet

The word of the Lord came to Jonah a second time, saying, 'Get up, go to Nineveh, that great city, and proclaim to it the message that I tell you.' So Jonah set out and went to Nineveh, according to the word of the Lord. Now Nineveh was an exceedingly large city, a three days' walk across. Jonah began to go into the city, going a day's walk. And he cried out, 'Forty days more, and Nineveh shall be overthrown!' And the people of Nineveh believed God; they proclaimed a fast, and everyone, great and small, put on sackcloth.

When the news reached the king of Nineveh, he rose from his throne, removed his robe, covered himself with sackcloth, and sat in ashes. Then he had a proclamation made in Nineveh: 'By the decree of the king and his nobles: No human being or animal, no herd or flock, shall taste anything. They shall not feed, nor shall they drink water. Human beings and animals shall be covered with sackcloth, and they shall cry mightily to God. All shall turn from their evil ways and from the violence that is in their hands. Who knows? God may relent and change his mind; he may turn from his fierce anger, so that we do not perish.'

When God saw what they did, how they turned from their

evil ways, God changed his mind about the calamity that he
had said he would bring upon them; and he did not do it.

But this was very displeasing to Jonah, and he became
angry. He prayed to the Lord and said, 'O Lord! Is not this
what I said while I was still in my own country? That is why
I fled to Tarshish at the beginning; for I knew that you are a
gracious God and merciful, slow to anger, and abounding in
steadfast love, and ready to relent from punishing. And now,
O Lord, please take my life from me, for it is better for me to
die than to live.'

JONAH 3:1—4:3

The story of Jonah, the prophet swallowed by a big fish, is
one of the best-known in the Old Testament. Although a
simple and entertaining tale, it carries a vital message. At
one level it is an amusing and satirical take on the prophet
Jonah, son of Amittai, who prophesied the expansion of the
borders of Israel under King Jeroboam II (2 Kings 14:25). At
another level, as we continue our Advent journey, we are
reminded that God's love and forgiveness are there for all
people, even the worst of sinners. The people of Israel are
God's chosen vehicle for conveying that message and for its
ultimate fulfilment in Christ, who died for the sins of the
whole world (1 John 2:2).

Nineveh was the capital of Assyria, one of the great empires
neighbouring Israel in ancient times—an aggressive expan-
sionist nation, brutally subduing the nations around it. It was
the Assyrians who conquered the northern kingdom of Israel.
To the Hebrews, therefore, Assyria was anathema, synony-
mous with the hated pagan empire that had destroyed Israel
and taken its citizens into exile. It was only by the grace of
God that the southern kingdom of Judah was spared a similar

fate until Nebuchadnezzar, king of Babylon, came along over a century later (2 Kings 24—25).

Jonah was the reluctant prophet sent to pronounce God's judgement on Nineveh, preaching probably the shortest sermon of all time: 'Forty days more, and Nineveh shall be overthrown!' (3:4). He was reluctant because he knew that if the Ninevites repented, then, far from destroying them, God would forgive them. Jonah knew that God is merciful, 'abounding in steadfast love' (4:2), and will even change his mind, not doing what he has previously declared he will do (3:10; see also Joel 2:12–14; Jeremiah 18:7–8). The Ninevites sensed this possibility too (3:9). The future is not cast in stone; it is not determined by our past misdeeds, but can be transformed by God's mercy.

The Ninevites, by command of their king, repented of the evil and violence they had committed. They fasted, put on sackcloth and ashes and agreed to 'cry mightily to God' (3:8). Even the cattle were included in this act of contrition. God heard them and was merciful.

The reason Jonah fled from God, ending up in the fish's belly, was that he did not want God to forgive the hated Ninevites. I wonder, do we regard anyone as 'beyond the pale', outside the reaches of God's forgiveness? Is there anyone who, we hope, might not be forgiven for the bad things they have done? Perhaps we can think of individuals—if not of our own acquaintance, then those who have committed the most horrific crimes—whom we think about in this way. God, however, is longing for them to come to repentance and receive his mercy and forgiveness. Indeed, it is God's desire that all should be saved and come to the knowledge of the truth (1 Timothy 2:4).

Jonah thought that his own people were God's chosen,

the apple of his eye—as indeed they were. However, he thought this meant that those outside the covenant community were excluded from God's love and concern, especially if they were Israel's enemies and behaved brutally towards Israel. He was wrong. God loves the Gentiles too, whom the people of Nineveh represent in the story. Jonah missed the point. The main purpose of God's covenant with Israel, from Abraham on, was to bless the whole world (Genesis 12:3).

Even today, we can think of ourselves in the church in a much too exclusive way. We can imagine that we are the ones God cares for and that those outside the community of faith don't matter. But God loves all people and it is our duty to proclaim the gospel of repentance and forgiveness and new life that come with faith in Christ. I hope we are not reluctant agents of God's message, like Jonah, but are eager to share the good news that God loves us and that even the worst of sinners can be welcomed into his kingdom.

Sometimes, though, it is not that we don't want people to hear the good news, but that we are afraid of what they will think of us, or we think it may be intrusive to raise issues of faith. The way we approach people will undoubtedly vary, and often we are better placed to speak of these fundamental issues when we have made genuine friendships with people. On the other hand, perhaps we need to recover some of the bluntness of Jonah's message and not be ultra-sensitive.

Jesus invoked the story of Jonah's mission to Nineveh in discussion with the Pharisees (Matthew 12:41). Jonah's sojourn in the fish's belly is a 'type' or symbol of Jesus' three days in the tomb. Moreover, Jesus is far greater than Jonah, so how much more should the people who witness his ministry repent than the Ninevites who merely heard the reluctant prophet. This too is a warning to us. We have heard the good news of Jesus and, I trust, responded to it. We need to persevere and live our lives in the light of this wonderful message of God's love and mercy. And let's not be reluctant prophets but enthusiastic about the wonderful good news we have to share.

For reflection and prayer

Ask yourself:

- *How eager or reluctant am I to approach others with the call to repentance and faith?*
- *Are there some people I don't want to help to receive God's forgiveness, perhaps because I have been hurt in some way in the past?*
- *How much courage do I have to challenge others and share my faith?*

Then you may like to pray as follows:

Lord Jesus, you gave your followers the command to go and make disciples of all nations. Forgive my reluctance to share the good news with those I know. Help me to proclaim the gospel of repentance, forgiveness and new life in Christ by my life, my deeds and my words, for your name's sake. Amen

How long, O Lord?

O God, why do you cast us off for ever?
Why does your anger smoke against the sheep
  of your pasture?
Remember your congregation, which you
  acquired long ago,
which you redeemed to be the tribe of your heritage.
Remember Mount Zion, where you came to dwell.
Direct your steps to the perpetual ruins;
the enemy has destroyed everything in the sanctuary.
Your foes have roared within your holy place;
they set up their emblems there.
At the upper entrance they hacked
the wooden trellis with axes.
And then, with hatchets and hammers,
they smashed all its carved work.
They set your sanctuary on fire;
they desecrated the dwelling-place of your name,
bringing it to the ground.
They said to themselves, 'We will utterly subdue them';
they burned all the meeting-places of God in the land.
We do not see our emblems;
there is no longer any prophet,
and there is no one among us who knows how long.
How long, O God, is the foe to scoff?

Is the enemy to revile your name for ever?
Why do you hold back your hand;
why do you keep your hand in your bosom?
Yet God my King is from of old,
working salvation in the earth.
You divided the sea by your might;
you broke the heads of the dragons in the waters.
You crushed the heads of Leviathan;
you gave him as food for the creatures of the wilderness.
You cut openings for springs and torrents;
you dried up ever-flowing streams.
Yours is the day, yours also the night;
you established the luminaries and the sun.
You have fixed all the bounds of the earth;
you made summer and winter.
Remember this, O Lord, how the enemy scoffs,
and an impious people reviles your name.
Do not deliver the soul of your dove to the wild animals;
do not forget the life of your poor for ever.
Have regard for your covenant,
for the dark places of the land are full of the
   haunts of violence.
Do not let the downtrodden be put to shame;
let the poor and needy praise your name.
Rise up, O God, plead your cause;
remember how the impious scoff at you all day long.
Do not forget the clamour of your foes,
the uproar of your adversaries that goes up continually.
PSALM 74

I have included this passage because one of the themes of
Advent is judgement. This is something we tend to shy away

from or feel uncomfortable about. Yet, as so often in the Psalms, the cry of the oppressed is heard here, and it is a cry for God to exercise judgement, a longing for God to put right what is wrong in the world. It is what many cry out for today: 'How long, O God, is the foe to scoff?' (v. 10).

In today's passage, the writer appeals to God's honour, since evil done against his people is evil done against God: 'Rise up, O God, plead your cause' (v. 22). The appeal is the more powerful since it is made to the all-powerful God. The God of the Hebrews is the God of creation (vv. 12–17); it is he who divided the sea and crushed the fearful sea monster Leviathan, which symbolises the powers of chaos; it is he who established day and night and the heavenly bodies to rule them; and it is he who made the seasons. This is clearly a God who can answer the prayers of his people.

The context for the psalm is probably the Babylonian exile. It gives a graphic description of the destruction of the temple in Jerusalem—for example, 'They set your sanctuary on fire' (v. 7). As Anthony Hanson puts it (writing about Revelation, but having equal relevance here), God's wrath consists partly in 'the working out in history of the consequences of men's sins'.[4] So, Judah sinned and the temple was destroyed and the people taken into exile. Judgement may have begun with God's people, in line with the warnings of the pre-exilic prophets, such as Amos. Nevertheless, woe to those who savagely treated God's chosen and beloved ones, on whom he would never give up! Babylon, the nation that committed the atrocities against Judah, was in its turn conquered, and King Cyrus of Persia permitted the Jews to return and rebuild their temple.

Sadly, the persecution of God's people, the Jews, has gone on down the centuries, most horrifically in Nazi Germany.

On Kristallnacht, 9 November 1938, the country's Jews were treated with terrifying brutality. At the time, Dietrich Bonhoeffer was working far away from his home in Berlin, illegally training pastors for the Confessing Church, the group of Christians who stood out against Nazism. He underlined verse 8 from this psalm in his Luther Bible, 'They burned all the meeting-places of God in the land', and wrote in the margin beside it '9.11.38'.[5] He also urged his seminarians to support the Jews, asking them to reflect on these words: 'He who touches you touches the apple of his eye' (Zechariah 2:8). The Nazi régime received the outworking of the consequences of its sins with the collapse and defeat of Germany in 1945.

The working out of divine judgement within history cannot, however, be the whole story. Scripture also recognises that cause and effect don't always operate so neatly, and, in any case, many innocent people suffer along the way. In Psalm 44:17–26, the psalmist argues with God, saying that his people have not forgotten him or violated the covenant. There has to be some final day of reckoning when justice will be done once and for all and the victims of injustice will be recompensed. The writers of the Old Testament surely had some sense that this was the case (Daniel 12 is perhaps the clearest prophecy of a final judgement).

The conclusive working out of divine judgement comes with Christ, who takes it upon himself on the cross. As Karl Barth says, he is 'the Judge judged in our place'.[6] This means that we can be acquitted in the heavenly court when he comes again to judge the world. It also means that all the sin and evil committed down the ages by human beings is taken up by him and defeated on the cross, in anticipation that it will be done away with for ever at his return. His kingdom of justice will mean a life of eternal joy in his presence for all who come to him in penitence and faith. There is even the opportunity of forgiveness and reconciliation for those who have committed the most terrible offences, as we saw when discussing Jonah.

We need to listen to the cry of the oppressed; many who are oppressed today are our Christian brothers and sisters. In the West we can feel too comfortable and fail to give much thought to the coming judgement. We need to support all who are suffering injustice, including those on our doorsteps as well as those far away, and we need to call on the oppressors to repent. We must do what we can, however little it seems, to bring about peace and reconciliation in the world. There will come a day of reckoning when all wrongs will be righted and peace and justice will reign supreme. Are we ourselves prepared for and longing for that day, as the prophets and psalmists of old longed for it?

For reflection

Do you know of a person or group suffering injustice? If so, what can you do to support their cause? If not, can you look for a local or international cause to support? Ask God for guidance as to how you might be involved.

14–20 DECEMBER

Turning to God's way

The future foreseen by the prophets is heralded by John the Baptist, who is symbolised by the third Advent candle. John appears in the Judean desert preaching a fiery message of baptism of repentance for the forgiveness of sins. He announces the arrival of one who is far greater, whom he points out as 'the Lamb of God'. This Lamb will be sacrificed to defeat sin and death, but he will also be the one who judges the world. Are we to be acquitted or condemned in his heavenly court?

The forerunner

The beginning of the good news of Jesus Christ, the Son of God. As it is written in the prophet Isaiah,

'See, I am sending my messenger ahead of you,
who will prepare your way;
the voice of one crying out in the wilderness:
"Prepare the way of the Lord,
make his paths straight."'

John the baptiser appeared in the wilderness, proclaiming a baptism of repentance for the forgiveness of sins. And people from the whole Judean countryside and all the people of Jerusalem were going out to him, and were baptised by him in the river Jordan, confessing their sins.

MARK 1:1–5

Today we celebrate John the Baptist, the last of the prophets and the one who heralds the arrival of the Messiah. As forerunner of the Messiah, John fulfils Old Testament prophecy himself, and there are many Old Testament allusions and quotations in today's passage. Indeed, while verse 3 is from Isaiah 40:3, verse 2 combines Exodus 23:20 with Malachi 3:1. In Exodus, the messenger, or angel, is to go before the Israelites as they journey towards the promised land. For Christians, the promised land, the land of milk and honey, is a picture in the here and now of eternal life in the kingdom of God, which we enter and enjoy for ever because Christ has come and lived among us, died our death and risen again.

The Malachi quotation is even more striking. This time the messenger precedes the Lord himself, who will suddenly come to his temple. The merest hint of an Old Testament quotation would have conjured up the whole context for the first hearers or readers of the text, who would have been familiar with their Hebrew scriptures. In this case there is a message of judgement: 'he is like a refiner's fire' (Malachi 3:2). There is a need for God's people to be refined and purified and to present right offerings to God, and John's message is one of repentance and baptism for the forgiveness of sins.

As at the beginning of our Advent journey, there is an urgency here, which is even more pronounced because the arrival of the Messiah is now imminent. Jesus is about to appear on the scene, to be baptised by John, and our Advent journey will culminate in ten days' time with the celebration of Christmas. Let us, then, redouble our preparations to meet the Messiah, our judge. Have we been examining ourselves, as I suggested we might at the beginning of this book? What have we found? If God has been showing us our imperfections and sins, we should repent, if we have not done so already. Perhaps we could consider some degree of fasting or abstinence as an additional way of focusing on God as we await our redemption. After all, once he arrives, we shall want to celebrate, to turn our fasting into feasting, to be able to welcome him with joy.

The Isaiah passage, too, states explicitly that it is the Lord's way that is being prepared. The context into which these words were spoken was the Babylonian exile. It seems to me, as I mentioned when discussing Isaiah 9:2–7 (8 December), that scriptural prophecy often has a double meaning. There is the immediate meaning and partial fulfilment for those who hear it, and a deeper meaning, in expectation of a final and complete fulfilment in the distant future. The prophet may or may not be aware of the latter meaning. The New Testament, and Jesus himself, gives us licence to see that fulfilment in his own person.

In Isaiah 40, God is about to do something new for his captive people. Just as he led them out of captivity in Egypt, so he is going to lead them out of exile in Babylon and back to their homeland. There they are to rebuild the temple (destroyed by King Nebuchadnezzar) and worship God in spirit and in truth. God brings about this return from exile through a pagan ruler, Cyrus the Great, king of Persia. Cyrus is even called Messiah, meaning 'anointed' (Isaiah 45:1). That is the immediate meaning of the passage. I was intrigued, as a scientist studying theology, to visit the British Museum and see how these events are confirmed for us from outside the Bible on the so-called 'Cyrus cylinder' held there, a declaration of the king's reforms dating from the end of the exilic period.

The deeper truth in this passage from Isaiah is revealed in the ministries of John the Baptist and Jesus. Tom Wright argues that, in Jesus' day, the Jews regarded themselves as being still in exile. They were back in their own land, but had not been fully restored. There was still much to come: 'the real return from exile, including the resurrection from the dead, is taking place, in an extremely paradoxical fashion, in Jesus' own ministry'.[7] These Old Testament prophecies are being fulfilled, but in a most surprising and, indeed, paradoxical way.

Through Jesus we have been brought back from our self-imposed exile, our alienation from God, into his kingdom of justice, peace and love. We experience that restoration now. However, it is still the case that 'here we have no lasting city, but we are looking for the city that is to come' (Hebrews 13:14). We therefore look for the completion at Jesus' second coming of what he began at his first, as we await the new creation when 'death will be no more; mourning and crying and pain will be no more, for the first things have passed away' (Revelation 21:4).

For reflection

How can I be ready to meet the Messiah, my Judge?

Advent used to be a 'little Lent', a 40-day period of abstinence before Christmas. Surrounded nowadays by so much early feasting, can I fast to some degree? Can I perhaps miss a meal or abstain from a TV programme or an hour at the computer, using that time to be quiet in God's presence to prepare the way of the Lord?

The way of humility

Now John was clothed with camel's hair, with a leather belt around his waist, and he ate locusts and wild honey. He proclaimed, 'The one who is more powerful than I is coming after me; I am not worthy to stoop down and untie the thong of his sandals. I have baptised you with water; but he will baptise you with the Holy Spirit.'

In those days Jesus came from Nazareth of Galilee and was baptised by John in the Jordan. And just as he was coming up out of the water, he saw the heavens torn apart and the Spirit descending like a dove on him. And a voice came from heaven, 'You are my Son, the Beloved; with you I am well pleased.'

MARK 1:6–11

One of the interesting things about John is his clothing, which recalls that of Elijah: 'a hairy man, with a leather belt around his waist' (2 Kings 1:8). The very last two verses of the Old Testament say, 'Lo, I will send you the prophet Elijah before the great and terrible day of the Lord comes. He will turn the hearts of parents to their children and the hearts of children to their parents, so that I will not come and strike the land with a curse' (Malachi 4:5–6).

Thus the Jews expected Elijah to return before the Messiah came. To this day, at Passover, Jewish families put an extra cup of wine out for Elijah. They are still longing and waiting for the fulfilment of their hopes. Poignantly, they say at the end of the meal, 'Next year in Jerusalem!' as they still look forward to their return from exile. Jesus, however, tells us that John the Baptist *is* 'Elijah who is to come' (Matthew 11:14; 17:10–13). Again, the scriptures are being fulfilled in a surprising and paradoxical way. John is not the same person as Elijah, but he goes 'with the spirit and power of Elijah' (Luke 1:17); the real Elijah appears on the mount of transfiguration (Matthew 17:3). John plays the role in the New Testament that Elijah played in the Old, and there are many parallels between the two, not least Elijah's rebuking of King Ahab compared with John's rebuking of Herod (1 Kings 18:17–18; compare Mark 6:17–18). The fact that Elijah *has* come means that the final fulfilment—the end to exile, the 'day of the Lord'—is about to take place. But who will believe it? Will we, 2000 years on, believe it, joyfully embrace it and make it our own?

In today's passage, John points to Jesus as the one whose sandals 'I am not worthy to stoop down and untie' (v. 7). John's humility is a lesson to us all. People flocked to him, hungry to hear and keen to repent, and this huge popularity could have gone to his head. Perhaps John was tempted to resent Jesus' taking centre stage, yet he accepted the role that God wanted him to fulfil. Jesus, too, though he was God incarnate, sat light to the supreme honour that he merited. He humbled himself and became the servant of all (Philippians 2:7), washing his disciples' feet (John 13:5) and bearing the pain and ignominy of a criminal's execution—for our sake.

Jesus' own humility is particularly evident in his being baptised by John. Yesterday we read that John preached 'a baptism of repentance for the forgiveness of sins' (Mark 1:4). Why, then, should Jesus, who is sinless, be baptised? I think it is because he identifies totally with the human condition; he really becomes 'one of us'. He identifies with sinners and takes their sin, their alienation from God, upon himself. As Jürgen Moltmann puts it, referring to Jesus' cry of dereliction on the cross (Mark 15:34: 'My God, my God, why have you forsaken me?'), Jesus shares our 'godforsakenness', as, astonishingly and in a mystery beyond our human comprehension, the persons of the Trinity are rent apart at the moment when Christ dies for the sins of the world.[8]

Humility is a Christian virtue that Christ exemplifies and exhorts us to practise (Matthew 5:5), but it is not one that the world respects. Rather, many people take pride in touting their achievements. Again, as we journey through Advent, this is an area of our lives we should examine. Are we proud, like the world, boasting in our achievements, our wealth, our house, our car—whatever it might be? Or, like Paul, is there just one thing we are able to boast of—the cross of Christ (Galatians 6:14)?

Jesus comes up out of the water; immediately the Holy Spirit descends on him and the heavenly voice proclaims his identity. The one who has so humbly submitted to John's baptism is none other than the Son of God. And here it isn't just Mark, the Gospel writer, telling us this (as he did in 1:1), but God the Father himself, speaking from heaven.

Jesus is God's Son by nature—in the words of the Nicene Creed, 'eternally begotten of the Father, God from God, Light from Light, true God from true God, begotten not made, of one Being with the Father'. The amazing thing is that, by taking human flesh, he makes us God's children and his own brothers and sisters by adoption (Galatians 4:5), and the Holy

Spirit who descended on him descends on us to make us like him. I hope you are as thrilled as I am by these astonishing gospel truths!

For reflection

Reflect on the following questions.

- *Do I feel dissatisfied with my roles in life?*
- *Do I feel I've been dealt a rough deal?*
- *Do I resent others taking the limelight or praise that I think I deserve, or do I accept the roles and gifts God has given me, no matter how lowly?*
- *Jesus washed his disciples' feet: what humble task can I perform this week for one of the least of his brothers or sisters?*

Pointing to the Saviour

This took place in Bethany across the Jordan where John was baptising.

The next day he saw Jesus coming towards him and declared, 'Here is the Lamb of God who takes away the sin of the world! This is he of whom I said, "After me comes a man who ranks ahead of me because he was before me." I myself did not know him; but I came baptising with water for this reason, that he might be revealed to Israel.' And John testified, 'I saw the Spirit descending from heaven like a dove, and it remained on him. I myself did not know him, but the one who sent me to baptise with water said to me, "He on whom you see the Spirit descend and remain is the one who baptises with the Holy Spirit." And I myself have seen and have testified that this is the Son of God.'

The next day John again was standing with two of his disciples, and as he watched Jesus walk by, he exclaimed, 'Look, here is the Lamb of God!'

JOHN 1:28–36

As a scientist, I am always interested in how we can place the biblical narrative in its geographical and historical setting. Of course, we recognise that scripture contains many different kinds of literature and not all of it is meant to be read literally and historically. Most scholars would argue that the Gospel of John was written towards the very end of the first century and contains the reflection of the church on the person of Christ: it is therefore less concerned with historical detail than the other three, so-called Synoptic Gospels. This may well be broadly correct, yet it is interesting that John gives certain geographical and historical indications which are not present in the other Gospels. One here is the reference to 'Bethany across the Jordan, where John was baptising' (v. 28).

In 2013 my wife led a pilgrimage tour to Jordan, and one of our visits was to the site most probably to be identified with Bethany across the Jordan. Clearly this site was deemed important to the early church, since the remains of three Byzantine churches are found there, built to commemorate John's baptising of Jesus. Interestingly, it is also near the place where Elijah is said to have been carried into heaven in a whirlwind (2 Kings 2:11). As we saw yesterday, John is the new Elijah. He is proclaimed as such by Jesus himself (Matthew 11:14), even though, in the verses preceding today's passage, the Baptist himself refuses to accept this identification (John 1:21).

It was a deeply moving experience to be in this place of pilgrimage. We saw a group of Orthodox Christians on the Israeli side of the river, undergoing full immersion baptisms. Our group held a Communion service, during which we renewed our baptismal vows, dipping our fingers in Jordan water and signing each other with the cross. Of course, in one sense it doesn't really matter precisely where John was baptising or if Jesus was baptised on this spot, and our weekly Eucharist in church at home is as valid as any other. At the same time, there is something very special about being on pilgrimage to holy sites with fellow Christians and celebrating the founding events of our faith *in situ*. Although our group was very diverse, we gelled together wonderfully well because of our common purpose in being there.

As I mentioned in the reading for 2 December, in 2002 I had the privilege of spending seven months as Chaplain of the English Church in Heidelberg, Germany. One of the most memorable trips we made from Heidelberg was to the town of Colmar, just over the French border in Alsace. The Musée Unterlinden in Colmar contains a famous painting known as the Isenheim altarpiece. Painted by Matthias Grünewald between 1512 and 1516, it depicts, unusually for its time, a harrowing, twisted and bloody picture of Christ on the cross, his body covered in sores. The painting was displayed by monks to patients suffering from St Anthony's fire, a terrible disease that wracked the body in the way Christ's body was wracked in the painting. The sufferers would have seen it every day when they came into the chapel for services. It is a picture of Christ truly entering into our own human sufferings and thereby bringing redemption. It depicts Christ directly fulfilling the prophecy we looked at last week: 'Surely he has borne our infirmities and carried our diseases; yet we accounted him stricken, struck down by God, and afflicted' (Isaiah 53:4).

My point today, however, is to note that to the right of the picture we see John the Baptist, with an exaggerated, elongated index finger pointing to the tortured figure of Christ. Written behind John in Latin are the words 'He must increase, but I must decrease' (John 3:30). The great Swiss theologian Karl Barth kept a reproduction of this painting hung above his desk for the 50 years of his work as a pastor and theologian. Particularly important to him was the portrayal of John the

Baptist and his pointing finger, which provided a suitable reminder of the task of the theologian. Like John, a theologian must point away from himself to Christ. Of course, in pointing to Christ, John is a model for all Christians, whether professional theologians or not.

In today's passage, John points to Jesus as 'the Lamb of God who takes away the sin of the world' (v. 29). The imagery brings to mind the whole system of animal sacrifice, which, the writer to the Hebrews tells us, was ultimately of no avail. In contrast, the one supreme sacrifice of Christ is effective in expiating the long catalogue of human misdeeds. How can we possibly thank God enough when we recognise that this is what it took, and how can we fail to point our friends and neighbours to this extraordinary gift to us of God's own Son? As we go deeper into Christ in our own spiritual journeys this Advent, let us remember the fact that, as William Temple put it, the 'Church is the only society on earth that exists for the benefit of non-members', and let us invite our friends to share the joy we have.

For reflection

You can find the Isenheim altarpiece here (click on the + sign to enlarge it): www.musee-unterlinden.com/altarpiece-with-wings-closed-the-crucifixion.html.

You may like to use this picture as an aid to meditation. As you look at it, repeat slowly John's words, 'Here is the Lamb of God who takes away the sin of the world! … He must increase, but I must decrease.' Think of ways you can point people to Jesus.

Doubts creep in

When John heard in prison what the Messiah was doing, he sent word by his disciples and said to him, 'Are you the one who is to come, or are we to wait for another?' Jesus answered them, 'Go and tell John what you hear and see: the blind receive their sight, the lame walk, the lepers are cleansed, the deaf hear, the dead are raised, and the poor have good news brought to them. And blessed is anyone who takes no offence at me.'

MATTHEW 11:2–6

The Gospels tell us that John was imprisoned because he criticised Herod Antipas for marrying Herodias, the wife of his half-brother Philip (Matthew 14:3–12). These brothers, Herod Antipas and Herod Philip, were sons of Herod the Great (the king of Judea at the time of Jesus' birth) by different wives. Herodias was also their niece, being the daughter of Aristobulus, their brother whom Herod the Great had commanded to be strangled. The internecine bloodletting and wife-stealing in this real-life historical dynasty was truly horrific. The portrayal of the Wars of the Roses in *The White Queen*, adapted from the novel by Philippa Gregory and running on British TV as I write, is not dissimilar to these goings-on. Indeed, there is much gritty realism in the

Bible. As Elijah stood up to King Ahab and his apostate wife Jezebel, earlier models of tyranny and violence, so John, the new Elijah, stands up to Herod and Herodias.

My scientific training often leads me to ask whether there is any evidence for what the Bible says from outside the text. Josephus tells us that John the Baptist was imprisoned in the fortress of Herod Antipas at Machaerus, and on our pilgrimage to Jordan in 2013 we visited this very fortress. Its remains lie on a remote hilltop east of the Dead Sea, and it was used by Herod the Great to fortify his possessions east of the River Jordan.

Josephus tells us that when Antipas's first wife got wind of his plans to divorce her and marry Herodias, she returned to her father, Aretas, king of Petra, who went to war with Herod over it. (This is the same King Aretas IV from whose governor in Damascus Paul escaped by being let down in a basket: see 2 Corinthians 11:32–33.) Aretas destroyed Herod's army and some of the Jews thought that this was God's judgement on Herod for what he had done against John. As the historian Josephus wrote, 'for he slew him, who was a good man, and commanded the Jews to exercise virtue, both as to righteousness towards one another, and piety towards God, and so to come to baptism'.[9] Josephus reckons that Herod was frightened that John might raise a rebellion, given his power over the people.

This corroborative detail from extra-biblical sources is interesting and exciting. But today we are confronted with the forerunner of the Messiah—the last and greatest prophet of all, Elijah who was to come—apparently wavering in his belief, just when, from our perspective, everything was being fulfilled. John seems to doubt that he was right after all, and this is not surprising. His prison was probably a cave below

Machaerus, and it would have felt very bleak and lonely to be incarcerated there.

This wasn't what John expected. It had seemed as though the longing and waiting were over, and all that remained was to believe. But then, in prison, nagging doubts arise in his mind, so he sends his disciples to Jesus to find out the truth of the matter.

I have been reading the profoundly moving book *Leaving Alexandria*, by former Bishop of Edinburgh, Richard Holloway.[10] Holloway is haunted by a strong sense of failure, of letting people and God down, as he has struggled with his weaknesses and doubts throughout his life. When doubts arise in our own minds, as they will do sometimes in all our lives, we can be reassured by the realism of the biblical record. The father of a dumb epileptic boy cried to Jesus, 'I believe; help my unbelief!' (Mark 9:24). Thomas famously doubted when told by his friends about Jesus' resurrection. Surely John the Baptist had everything going for him in terms of believing that Jesus was the Messiah—the circumstances of his own birth, the message he preached, the scriptural passages supporting all of this, and, perhaps especially, his own personal knowledge of his cousin Jesus whom he had baptised—yet John doubted as we do.

In the Old Testament, the Hebrews were encouraged, when in trouble and doubt, to look back at the great things God had done in creation and in bringing them out of slavery in Egypt. Jesus points John's disciples to what he himself is doing in the present. He is fulfilling Old Testament prophecy in a remarkable way: 'Then the eyes of the blind shall be opened, and the ears of the deaf unstopped; then the lame shall leap like a deer, and the tongue of the speechless sing for joy' (Isaiah 35:5–6). Perhaps John had not realised he should expect just these signs of fulfilment. Maybe he was too focused on the judgement that the Messiah would bring (Matthew 3:12), important though that is, and missed the mercy—the idea that the coming of the Messiah is good news for the poor and suffering (Isaiah 61:1–4). Maybe, too, John shared some of his Jewish co-religionists' expectations that the Messiah would oust tyrants like Herod and the Roman occupiers. But I am sure John would have recognised the signs Jesus was performing when he was told about them by his disciples. I pray that, when our circumstances are hard, we too will take comfort from what God has done in the past and will recognise what he is doing right now.

For prayer

Lord Jesus Christ, you have taken away the sin of the world and are alive for ever more. When I doubt, please help me to believe the truth in your word and to wait for you to show me the way ahead, for your name's sake. Amen

Thank God that he never leaves you, but rather carries you when you are going through tough times: 'Be strong and courageous; do not be frightened or dismayed, for the Lord your God is with you wherever you go' (Joshua 1:9); 'Blessed be the Lord, who daily bears us up; God is our salvation' (Psalm 68:19).

Death defeated

Listen, I will tell you a mystery! We will not all die, but we will all be changed, in a moment, in the twinkling of an eye, at the last trumpet. For the trumpet will sound, and the dead will be raised imperishable, and we will be changed. For this perishable body must put on imperishability, and this mortal body must put on immortality. When this perishable body puts on imperishability, and this mortal body puts on immortality, then the saying that is written will be fulfilled:

'Death has been swallowed up in victory.'
'Where, O death, is your victory?
Where, O death, is your sting?'

The sting of death is sin, and the power of sin is the law. But thanks be to God, who gives us the victory through our Lord Jesus Christ. Therefore, my beloved, be steadfast, immovable, always excelling in the work of the Lord, because you know that in the Lord your labour is not in vain.

1 CORINTHIANS 15:51–58

Death is a taboo subject in much of today's society. We are far more shielded from it than past generations ever were. Our average life expectancy is much greater than in the past, and, unless they die in distant war zones or natural disasters, people tend to die in sanitised surroundings in hospital. So we don't tend to see death at first hand, except when finally sitting with a loved one who passes away on a hospital bed.

Death is something that frightens people, and perhaps that is why they do not talk about it. These days there is much less certainty about any kind of afterlife and therefore many more people see death as the end.

In the Old Testament, death is the natural end of life and only really to be regretted if it is premature. So it is a great blessing to die 'full of years' (see, for example, Genesis 25:8). There is very little hint of resurrection, the first clear instance being in Daniel 12:2, which is very late, having been written during the Maccabean period (second century BC). Instead, the Old Testatment speaks of 'Sheol', the rather bleak place of the dead. The word is translated into Greek as Hades, familiar from classical literature as the realm of the shades of the departed. In some passages it denotes abandonment by God to a place of corruption (Isaiah 14:11; 38:18; Psalm 16:8–11; compare Acts 2:25–28), although elsewhere we find that God can be present even there (Psalm 139:8).

In the light of Christ's death and resurrection, death is completely transformed. It is not something to be feared; it is the gateway from the perishable nature of our present existence to the imperishable, from the mortal to immortality. When we say in the creed, 'He descended into hell [Hades]', we are affirming that Christ went there on our behalf; he suffered our death so that we may pass from death to his resurrection life, 'in the twinkling of an eye'.

Today's passage is not sentimental about death, however. It does not say 'Death is nothing at all', as is so commonly read at funerals these days. No, death is real and brings great grief to those who mourn. Earlier in this chapter Paul calls it 'the last enemy to be destroyed' (1 Corinthians 15:26). Using Old

Testament quotations to make his point, Paul taunts defeated death: 'Death has been swallowed up in victory. Where, O death, is your victory? Where, O death, is your sting?' (see Isaiah 25:8; Hosea 13:14).

Paul says that the sting of death is sin, which makes death much more dreadful than it otherwise would be. Sin is what makes death something to be feared. Will death mean judgement and facing the consequences of being found wanting, or will it mean forgiveness and new hope and joy? Even if we anticipate the latter, death can also bring regrets and feelings of guilt. Have I wasted my life? Have I harmed others? Are there people I am not reconciled with? Have I loved and been loved or have I detached myself from the commitment that love requires, for fear of being hurt? The 2007 film *The Bucket List* is a moving portrayal of two dying men who compile a list of things they want do to before they die. Through their experience of ticking off items on their 'bucket list', each discovers the most important thing he needs to learn—one, that he loves his wife, and the other, that he should be reconciled with his daughter.

In addition, Paul tells us that the power of sin is the law. To understand this, we need to refer to his teaching about the law in Romans 7: the law is holy, good and spiritual but it shows up sin for what it is (vv. 12–14). For example, Paul would not have known what it meant to covet if the law had not said, 'You shall not covet.' Thus the law sharpens our sense of moral culpability, and, as we face death, it makes our sense of failure and regret that much greater. But in today's passage Paul shows us that we can rejoice because Jesus has conquered sin and death, and we can declare triumphantly, 'Thanks be to God, who gives us the victory through our Lord Jesus Christ' (1 Corinthians 15:57).

Does the hope of resurrection mean that we neglect the world? Far from it. Paul tells us that, in the light of Christ's victory, we should be 'always excelling in the work of the Lord, because you know that in the Lord your labour is not in vain' (v. 58).

For Dietrich Bonhoeffer, the Christian hope of the resurrection certainly does not absolve the Christian from concern for this world. Rather, it 'sends a man back to his life on earth in a wholly new way'. This means that the Christian has to face earthly tasks and difficulties head on, because 'only in his doing so is the crucified and risen Lord with him, and he crucified and risen with Christ'.[11] Bonhoeffer undoubtedly drank his own earthly tasks to the dregs. Executed for his part in the German resistance movement, his last recorded words, on being led to the scaffold, were full of tremendous hope: 'This is the end—for me the beginning of life.'[12]

For reflection

*Then said he, I am going to my Father's, and though with great Difficulty I am got hither, yet now I do not repent me of all the Trouble I have been at to arrive where I am. **My Sword** I give to him that shall succeed me in my Pilgrimage; and my **Courage** and **Skill** to him that can get it. My **Marks** and **Scars** I carry with me, to be a Witness for me, that I have fought his Battles, who now will be my Rewarder. When the Day that he must go hence, was come, many accompanied him to the River side, into which as he went he said, **Death, where is thy Sting?** And as he went down deeper, he said, **Grave, where is thy Victory?** So he passed over, and all the Trumpets sounded for him on the other side.*

MR VALIANT-FOR-TRUTH, IN JOHN BUNYAN'S *THE PILGRIM'S PROGRESS*[13]

Serving Christ in others

'When the Son of Man comes in his glory, and all the angels with him, then he will sit on the throne of his glory. All the nations will be gathered before him, and he will separate people one from another as a shepherd separates the sheep from the goats, and he will put the sheep at his right hand and the goats at the left. Then the king will say to those at his right hand, "Come, you that are blessed by my Father, inherit the kingdom prepared for you from the foundation of the world; for I was hungry and you gave me food, I was thirsty and you gave me something to drink, I was a stranger and you welcomed me, I was naked and you gave me clothing, I was sick and you took care of me, I was in prison and you visited me." Then the righteous will answer him, "Lord, when was it that we saw you hungry and gave you food, or thirsty and gave you something to drink? And when was it that we saw you a stranger and welcomed you, or naked and gave you clothing? And when was it that we saw you sick or in prison and visited you?" And the king will answer them, "Truly I tell you, just as you did it to one of the least of these who are members of my family, you did it to me." Then he will say to those at his left hand, "You that are accursed, depart from me into the eternal fire prepared for the devil and his angels; for I was hungry and you gave me no food, I was thirsty and you gave me nothing to drink, I was a stranger and you did not welcome me, naked and you did not give me clothing, sick and in prison and you did not visit me." Then they also will answer, "Lord, when was it that we saw you hungry or thirsty or a stranger or naked or sick or in prison, and did not take care of you?" Then he will answer them, "Truly I tell you, just as you did not do it to one of the least of these, you did not do it to me." And these will go away into eternal punishment, but the righteous into eternal life.'

MATTHEW 25:31–46

In this passage Jesus paints a picture of the last judgement. The judge is the Son of Man, the title Jesus took for himself, based on the figure in Daniel 7:13–14 who comes 'with the clouds' to the 'Ancient of Days' and is given everlasting dominion over all peoples. He separates the nations into sheep and goats and judges them by what they have done. Have they fed Jesus when he was hungry or visited him in prison or welcomed him in the guise of a stranger?

Who are Jesus' 'family' (v. 40) to whom all this service is done? Are they Christians or all people? You can argue either way. Certainly, the way people react to Jesus and the message of his love conveyed by his disciples is of vital importance. Ultimately this is what our salvation hinges on. Other passages in Matthew's Gospel seem to support the idea that service to his disciples is service to Jesus (for example, 10:40–42). On the other hand, the word 'family' (Greek 'brothers') is omitted in 25:45, and Jesus generally teaches that we should love all people. This understanding has inspired Christians to serve the poor and destitute down the ages. Since humans are made in the image of God, each one is of infinite value and concern—to God and therefore to us.

Jesus is talking here to his disciples and is primarily concerned to teach us about how we should treat other people, but this is also a passage about judgement, a theme we keep returning to during Advent. We may rejoice that the righteous go to eternal life, but we may also find it disturbing that those who do not minister to Jesus in others are banished to 'the eternal fire prepared for the devil and his angels' (v. 41). Can Jesus, the Lamb of God who died for the sins of the world, really consign people to eternal punishment?

As I see it, there are a number of truths we need to hold together here. First, as so often in scripture and especially in apocalyptic visions of the end, this is picture language. The picture of eternal hell-fire is surely a metaphor for that most tragic of possible states, irredeemable separation from God. Second, in the new creation, peace, justice and love will reign supreme. Nothing evil can continue to coexist with the good (Revelation 21:27); all will be purity and truth and light. Third, God's desire is for 'everyone to be saved and to come to the knowledge of the truth' (1 Timothy 2:4). In dying on the cross for the sins of the whole world, Jesus has done all that is necessary for that to come about (1 John 2:2). However, in the end it may still be possible to reject God's love. Some people may turn in on themselves, in spite and hatred, so far as to render themselves beyond redemption. A person who has never heard of Jesus cannot be rejecting salvation, but if someone makes a conscious and self-willed decision to reject God's love, God will honour that choice. Tragic as this is, it is a possibility that we cannot exclude. As C.S. Lewis puts it in his masterful allegory on the subject of heaven and hell, *The Great Divorce*, 'There are only two kinds of people in the end: those who say to God, "Thy will be done," and those to whom God says, in the end, "*Thy* will be done." All that are in Hell, choose it.'[14]

For us the message is clear. We are to serve all people as if they were Jesus. The Russian novelist Leo Tolstoy tells a beautiful and moving Christmas story about a village shoemaker, Papa Panov.[15] On Christmas Eve, Papa Panov reads in his Bible that there was no room for Mary and Joseph in the inn, and he has a dream in which Jesus promises to come to him the next day. He is naturally very excited at this prospect and plans to welcome Jesus properly. Throughout Christmas Day he watches for his special visitor. A few people do come. One is the road sweeper, who is only too pleased to come in from the cold and drink Papa Panov's proffered cup of coffee. Another is a poor young mother with her child. Papa Panov warms some milk and finds shoes for the child—the very best shoes he has ever made, which he had been keeping for Jesus.

At the end of the day, Papa Panov puts up the shutters, disappointed that the visitor he really hoped for hasn't come after all, but suddenly he knows he is not alone in the room. At first he sees the people he had met that day passing by, and each whispers, 'Didn't you see *me*, Papa Panov?' Then he hears the voice of Jesus: 'I was hungry and you fed me. I was naked and you clothed me. I was cold and you warmed me. I came to you today in every one of those you helped and welcomed.'

Can we discern the image of Jesus in those around us in need? I pray that we can.

For prayer

Blessed are you, Sovereign God of all,
to you be praise and glory for ever.
In your tender compassion
the dawn from on high is breaking upon us
to dispel the lingering shadows of night.
As we look for your coming among us this day,
open our eyes to behold your presence
and strengthen our hands to do your will,
that the world may rejoice and give you praise.

OPENING PRAYER OF THANKS FOR ADVENT AT MORNING PRAYER,
COMMON WORSHIP [16]

20 DECEMBER

Will all be saved?

Blessed be the God and Father of our Lord Jesus Christ, who has blessed us in Christ with every spiritual blessing in the heavenly places, just as he chose us in Christ before the foundation of the world to be holy and blameless before him in love. He destined us for adoption as his children through Jesus Christ, according to the good pleasure of his will, to the praise of his glorious grace that he freely bestowed on us in the Beloved. In him we have redemption through his blood, the forgiveness of our trespasses, according to the riches of his grace that he lavished on us. With all wisdom and insight he has made known to us the mystery of his will, according to his good pleasure that he set forth in Christ, as a plan for the fullness of time, to gather up all things in him, things in heaven and things on earth. In Christ we have also obtained an inheritance, having been destined according to the purpose of him who accomplishes all things according to his counsel and will, so that we, who were the first to set our hope on Christ, might live for the praise of his glory. In him you also, when you had heard the word of truth, the gospel of your salvation, and had believed in him, were marked with the seal of the promised Holy Spirit; this is the pledge of our inheritance towards redemption as God's own people, to the praise of his glory.

EPHESIANS 1:3–14

In this purple passage Paul is almost falling over himself in praise of what God has done for us in Christ. I hope we can share his exuberance! We who are in Christ have been blessed with every spiritual blessing in the heavenly places and chosen before the foundation of the world to be holy and blameless before him. Before time and space ever were, God had a purpose. Through his Son, he desired to bring about a community who would be his children by adoption and grace. It is a truly astonishing thought.

We who belong to this community of the Church have been redeemed through the blood of Christ. We are forgiven, and this forgiveness is free—not something we could even possibly earn. It is the lavish gift of God's grace.

Martin Luther was deeply troubled by the righteousness of God, feeling that it was a standard he could never attain. Like Paul, he was bowled over when he discovered that the righteousness of God was, like forgiveness, God's free gift to him, to be received in faith. Even the faith to receive it was a gift (Ephesians 2:8)! This is what is meant by the great Reformation cries of 'sola gratia, sola fide'—'by grace alone, by faith alone'. We rely totally on what God has done for us in Christ. Therefore our 'works', our obedience to Jesus' commands, are not merits that could earn God's favour as a reward, but are the way in which we show our gratitude to God for his great grace.

God's amazing grace is wonderful good news, and Paul is encouraging Christians to recognise the sheer unmerited generosity of God towards them. Some Christians, however, have concluded from this passage that there is a parallel class of people who have been 'chosen before the foundation of the world' for damnation rather than salvation. That strikes me as hardly compatible with the infinitely loving and merciful God revealed in Jesus. Nevertheless, the question arises: will everyone be saved or not?

We cannot resolve this important issue in a brief reflection. Some passages of scripture seem to suggest that all will be saved (the universalist position).[17] Other passages indicate that it is God's will that all should be saved, but do not explicitly say that all will, in fact, be saved.[18] In today's passage we read that 'all things' will be gathered up or united in him, things in both heaven and earth (v. 10), which seems universalist. Likewise, in Colossians 1:20 God reconciles 'all things' to himself through Christ.

On the other hand, some passages, including yesterday's (Matthew 25:31–46), do seem to indicate that some will not be saved. Is that really the case, or is the purpose of that highly symbolic passage solely to challenge Christians to see Christ in others?

It may well be that there are paradoxes here that we cannot resolve this side of eternity. God's logic may be different from our logic, as indicated by C.S. Lewis in *The Great Divorce*, where the narrator's guide tells him that it is impossible to see eternity through the lens of time.[19] Lewis's final Narnia story, *The Last Battle*, is also helpful in showing how it might be possible for someone to choose death rather than life, darkness rather than light, hell rather than heaven. A group of dwarfs have come through a stable door and find themselves in the next life. However, they are imprisoned in their own minds. They cannot see the beauty all around them or taste the delicious food they are offered. They won't let the lion Aslan help them.[20] Miroslav Volf expresses it well: 'If evildoers experience God's terror, it will not be because they have done evil, but because they have resisted to the end the powerful lure of the open arms of the crucified Messiah.'[21]

An illustration from science may also be helpful. Quantum theory describes the behaviour of matter and energy at the scale of the very small, but quantum logic is very different from our ordinary everyday logic. In quantum theory, a particle can go through two slits in a screen at the same time—indeed, it can be in lots of places at once. We cannot study the world of the very small with our preconceived ideas of how things must logically be. Similarly, it may be that our everyday logic is inadequate and only God knows the answer to the riddles that puzzle us about human destiny. A humble approach is surely to remain somewhat agnostic on the matter, rather than thinking we have it all buttoned up, and to pray for those who do not know Jesus.

Let us, then, with Paul, praise God for the riches he bestows on us. Let us fulfil our destiny to 'live for the praise of his glory' (Ephesians 1:12), and let us thank God that we have been sealed with 'the promised Holy Spirit' (v. 13). The Greek word translated 'pledge' in verse 14 was used in commercial documents to mean 'deposit' or 'down payment' and it guaranteed the validity of a legal contract. The gift of the Spirit is therefore God's guarantee or pledge that more is to come—that one day we shall receive our inheritance in full. Surely no contract can be more secure than one made by God himself. How wonderful its fulfilment will be!

For prayer

Re-read today's passage, substituting 'I' and 'me' for 'we' and 'us', and thank God for his great gifts to you. Then pray for someone you know who is not yet aware of God's gift of salvation and ask God to give you opportunities to talk to your friend about Jesus.

Welcoming God's Son

BC turns to AD as a young woman is startled by an angelic visitor announcing that she is to be a virgin mother. How perplexing, not just for Mary, but for her devout husband-to-be, Joseph! Yet this child is the Son of God, the one in whom the promises to the patriarchs and the visions of the prophets are fulfilled. By his lowly birth and solidarity with the poor, he turns the values of the world upside down. As he took human nature, so we are enabled to participate in his divine nature. We light the fourth Advent candle to symbolise Mary.

Saying 'Yes' to God

In the sixth month the angel Gabriel was sent by God to a town in Galilee called Nazareth, to a virgin engaged to a man whose name was Joseph, of the house of David. The virgin's name was Mary. And he came to her and said, 'Greetings, favoured one! The Lord is with you.' But she was much perplexed by his words and pondered what sort of greeting this might be. The angel said to her, 'Do not be afraid, Mary, for you have found favour with God. And now, you will conceive in your womb and bear a son, and you will name him Jesus. He will be great, and will be called the Son of the Most High, and the Lord God will give to him the throne of his ancestor David. He will reign over the house of Jacob for ever, and of his kingdom there will be no end.' Mary said to the angel, 'How can this be, since I am a virgin?' The angel said to her, 'The Holy Spirit will come upon you, and the power of the Most High will overshadow you; therefore the child to be born will be holy; he will be called Son of God. And now, your relative Elizabeth in her old age has also conceived a son; and this is the sixth month for her who was said to be barren. For nothing will be impossible with God.' Then Mary said, 'Here am I, the servant of the Lord; let it be with me according to your word.' Then the angel departed from her.

LUKE 1:26–38

One of my favourite paintings is the famous *Annunciation* by Fra Angelico in the Monastery of San Marco, Florence. Each of the monks' cells displays one of Fra Angelico's frescoes and you see the *Annunciation* at the top of the stairs on the way to the cells. It is a very simple scene, with the angel and Mary just bending towards each other, looking into each other's eyes, each with crossed arms. It beautifully captures the moment of Mary's quiet acquiescence as the heavenly messenger announces that she is to bear God's Son. What a marvellous aid this and their individual frescoes would have been to the monks' contemplations!

Mary is at first troubled, and no wonder. She is a young girl, a virgin, not yet married to her fiancé, Joseph. How can she become pregnant before they come together in marriage? And what will Joseph, the respectable carpenter from Nazareth, think? How will her parents react? How will she face the accusations and rejection of the other villagers, who are likely to assume the worst of her?

What is amazing is that the angel's explanation satisfies her. This is to be God's Son, conceived miraculously by the power of the Holy Spirit. This is to be the ruler, the Messiah foretold by the prophets of old. However, God requires Mary's free acceptance. God is to come into the world he has created and will be 'despised and rejected by others' (Isaiah 53:3), but, from among those longing and waiting for him to come, he requires one to believe in the greatest miracle of all and to say 'Yes' to being part of it. Mary is the most significant human agent in the story of our salvation.

It seems to me that any attempt to look at what happened here scientifically only enhances the status of Jesus' conception as miraculous. For example, in nature, virgin birth (called 'parthenogenesis', from the Greek *parthenos* meaning 'virgin', the word used in today's passage) occurs in one in 1000 animal species, but the offspring are all female. Mary, as a normal girl, would have had two X chromosomes and no male Y chromosome to pass on (if she had had a Y chromosome she could have looked female but would have had some male characteristics and been sterile anyway). Here we simply have to recognise that God, the Lord of nature, is free to act outside the normal course of nature. This is not a problem to me as a scientist, and I shall have more to say about this tomorrow.

Mary's 'Yes' to becoming the mother of the Son of God is a model for our own response to God's call on our lives. Mary is called to be, quite literally, the bearer of God's Son. The archangel tells her that she is highly favoured and has been selected as God's chosen vessel to carry his Son: Christ is to be formed in her. We too are called to be Christ-bearers, to say 'Yes' to God and to allow the Son of God to be formed in us— as Paul puts it, 'Christ in you, the hope of glory' (Colossians 1:27). Jesus himself said, 'On that day you will know that I am in my Father, and you in me, and I in you' (John 14:20).

Dietrich Bonhoeffer expresses this truth in a characteristically radical way: 'The Church is not a religious community of worshippers of Christ but is Christ Himself who has taken form among men... The Church is nothing but a section of humanity in which Christ has really taken form.'[22] This is where the Church differs from any other human organisation. Bonhoeffer says that this isn't about applying Christ's teaching or Christian principles to the world, but about 'being drawn into the form of Jesus Christ'; it is about the form of Jesus Christ moulding our form in its own likeness.

Bonhoeffer goes on, 'It is not written that God became an idea, a principle, a programme, a universally valid proposition or a law, but that God became man.' Indeed, and that is what is happening in Mary, as she bears the incarnate Word, the eternal Son, in her womb from conception to birth, and cradles him in her arms. But it is to happen in us too! As the Christmas carol 'O little town of Bethlehem' says:

O holy child of Bethlehem,
Descend to us, we pray;
Cast out our sin, and enter in;
Be born in us today.
PHILLIPS BROOKS

If it is true that ideas can change the world, how much more true is it the case that Christ taking form in humanity can change the world? The incarnation was a one-off, a unique event, but when his people take his form and are shaped by him, Christ is taken with transforming power into every section and corner of society, to every town and every village, to every place where Christians are living and working.

What does your 'Yes' to God involve this Advent—indeed, this very day? Does the thought of Jesus Christ being born in you inspire you for his service, to do great things for him, to reach out to others who need to say 'Yes' to him too? Do you and your church see yourselves as 'Christ who has taken form among men'—the great transforming power in your own parish or community?

For reflection

You can find Fra Angelico's fresco of the Annunciation here (scroll down past the museum's plan and click on the image immediately below it): www.museumsinflorence.com/musei/museum_of_san_marco.html.

You could use this painting to meditate on Mary's saying 'Yes' to God. God is calling you to be a Christ-bearer. Will you say 'Yes' to Christ being formed in you? Will you be a Christ-bearer as you long and wait for his return in glory?

22 DECEMBER

Joseph's perspective

Now the birth of Jesus the Messiah took place in this way. When his mother Mary had been engaged to Joseph, but before they lived together, she was found to be with child from the Holy Spirit. Her husband Joseph, being a righteous man and unwilling to expose her to public disgrace, planned to dismiss her quietly. But just when he had resolved to do this, an angel of the Lord appeared to him in a dream and said, 'Joseph, son of David, do not be afraid to take Mary as your wife, for the child conceived in her is from the Holy Spirit. She will bear a son, and you are to name him Jesus, for he will save his people from their sins.' All this took place to fulfil what had been spoken by the Lord through the prophet: 'Look, the virgin shall conceive and bear a son, and they shall name him Emmanuel', which means, 'God is with us.' When Joseph awoke from sleep, he did as the angel of the Lord commanded him; he took her as his wife, but had no marital relations with her until she had borne a son; and he named him Jesus.

MATTHEW 1:18–25

Today we read the story of the virgin birth from Joseph's point of view. We can imagine Joseph's perplexity. He might well have been justifiably angry on learning that Mary was pregnant before their marriage and their coming together. Yet he showed real compassion for Mary in wanting to divorce her 'quietly'.

We are sometimes told that we can't possibly believe in the virgin birth in this scientific age. We know how babies are conceived and we know that virgin births just don't happen—at any rate, not in humans. Even if they did, as I pointed out yesterday, the offspring would invariably be female.

This argument is vulnerable at several points. First, science doesn't tell us what can and can't happen. It tells us how the *normal* pattern of cause and effect in the world operates. As a Christian, I would say that science shows God's normal pattern of working, through the regularity of natural law, and it shows God's faithfulness in sustaining a universe of order and predictability. If God were capriciously interfering with the laws of nature, it would be very hard for us to plan and live our lives in any kind of orderly way. Apart from anything else, it would be impossible for us to do science. So the regular working of the laws of nature demonstrates God's faithfulness to us and to his creation.

Of course, as the great theologians of the church have realised, that doesn't limit God. Thomas Aquinas, for example, makes a distinction between primary and secondary causes. God is the primary cause of all things—he causes them to exist in the first place and gives them the causal powers they have to act—but creatures can and do act as secondary causes, through the powers that God has given them.[23] Interestingly enough, Charles Darwin used this picture of secondary causes in explaining how natural selection works. Natural laws of all kinds simply describe the working of the secondary causes implanted in the natural order by God.

This idea of secondary causes does not limit God's action, because God freely created the secondary causes and they are subject to him. Moreover, he is free to act outside the order of secondary causes, as he would in the case of miracles.[24]

Another thing that's often said is that the people of the New Testament were unsophisticated peasants. They had no knowledge of modern science and were therefore quite happy to believe in extraordinary happenings, which they attributed to the action of God or the gods. But, as Tom Wright has pointed out about today's passage, 'Joseph was worried about Mary's unexpected pregnancy not because he did not know where babies come from but because he did.'[25] Joseph knew that as well as you and I know it, and that is why his suspicions were aroused.

I believe that we can and should believe in the virgin birth. For me, belief seems right because it fits with the rest of what scripture says about Jesus, including most especially his resurrection. The resurrection, for which there is excellent evidence, is what ultimately validates claims about who Jesus is—namely, the Son of God. There is also good reason to believe that the Gospel writers were generally reliable and truthful witnesses. Luke's preface to his Gospel says that he has written only 'after investigating everything carefully' (1:3). In other words, Luke has done his research. Matthew has trawled the Old Testament for quotations that he sees fulfilled in the events surrounding Jesus' nativity.

True, the Gospel writers are not neutral. They have an agenda and want to persuade us that what they say is true. Yet it seems to me that their accounts do ring true. They only write as they do because the early church has known and experienced Christ. It has witnessed his teaching and his miracles, has witnessed him alive 'by many convincing proofs' after his death (Acts 1:3), and is also convinced of his virgin birth.

While Joseph was mulling over what to do about Mary, he had a dream in which the true state of affairs was revealed to him. This changed everything: at last Joseph knew that Mary was innocent. Much more than that, she was specially favoured by God, and Joseph had the responsibility of being stepfather to the one whose name shall be Emmanuel, 'God with us' (Matthew 1:23). The longing and waiting of the Jewish nation and the whole world were in the hands of these Galilean peasants, who dared to believe in the promises of God.

Can we, too, dare to believe in God's promises, even if life seems to be going awry, as it was for Joseph when it looked as though his fiancée had been unfaithful? Let us take to heart what Paul says in Romans 8:28: 'We know that all things work together for good for those who love God, who are called according to his purpose.' God can and does bring good out of the direst and most unpromising circumstances.

For reflection

Joseph

No reason for travel.
No room for a bed.
No midwife at hand.
The responsibility so great—
such anxiety
no wonder.

The child—so frail, so perfect,
God's Son through Mary's 'yes',
of David's line through me.

Mine, though not mine
(what matter gossips' prattle now?),
To cherish, teach, protect
and love.
A great and mighty
wonder.

FROM 'SURRENDER AT THE CRIB', MALLING ABBEY

Believing God's promise

In those days Mary set out and went with haste to a Judean town in the hill country, where she entered the house of Zechariah and greeted Elizabeth. When Elizabeth heard Mary's greeting, the child leapt in her womb. And Elizabeth was filled with the Holy Spirit and exclaimed with a loud cry, 'Blessed are you among women, and blessed is the fruit of your womb. And why has this happened to me, that the mother of my Lord comes to me? For as soon as I heard the sound of your greeting, the child in my womb leapt for joy. And blessed is she who believed that there would be a fulfilment of what was spoken to her by the Lord.' And Mary said,

'My soul magnifies the Lord,
and my spirit rejoices in God my Saviour,
for he has looked with favour on the lowliness
   of his servant.
Surely, from now on all generations will call me blessed;
for the Mighty One has done great things for me,
and holy is his name.
His mercy is for those who fear him
from generation to generation.

He has shown strength with his arm;
he has scattered the proud in the thoughts of their hearts.
He has brought down the powerful from their thrones,
and lifted up the lowly;
he has filled the hungry with good things,
and sent the rich away empty.
He has helped his servant Israel,
in remembrance of his mercy,
according to the promise he made to our ancestors,
to Abraham and to his descendants for ever.'

And Mary remained with her for about three months and then returned to her home.

LUKE 1:39–56

In his Gospel, Luke has a particular focus and concern for the lower strata of society, who included the poor, the sick and, sad to say, in first-century Judea, women. Here are two pregnant women whom God has specially favoured, Mary and her cousin Elizabeth. Elizabeth's pregnancy, like Mary's, was miraculous. We are told that she was barren and both she and her husband, the priest Zechariah, were advanced in years. There are many echoes of Old Testament stories of God's grace here. As we saw at the beginning of our Advent journey, Abraham and his wife Sarah were both old when God promised them a son, and Isaac was the result. Hannah, wife of the Ephraimite Elkanah, was also barren, but God answered her prayer and she conceived and gave birth to the prophet Samuel (1 Samuel 1:1—2:10).

In these societies it was a great reproach for a married woman to be childless, besides the fact that a son was required to support his parents in their old age. Children were rightly seen as a sign of God's blessing (Psalm 127:3–5), but that could have an adverse effect on those who were childless. There seems to have been a more positive view of the childless woman later, in the century or so before Christ. For example, in the Apocryphal book Wisdom of Solomon, we read, 'For blessed is the barren woman who is undefiled... she will have fruit when God examines souls' (Wisdom 3:13). Nevertheless, in New Testament times, childlessness would still have been a hardship—a point implicitly understood when Jesus brought the son of the widow of Nain back to life (Luke 7:11–15). Thankfully, to be childless today does not carry the same stigma as in the past, but it is nevertheless deeply traumatic for those who would dearly love to have children, as my wife and I can testify from personal experience.

Elizabeth is to be the mother of John the Baptist, and Mary of the Messiah. The encounter between the two is intensely moving. The forerunner of the Messiah is at six months gestation in the womb and leaps for joy at the presence of his Lord, who is an embryo no more than a few cell divisions old at this point. It is a truly astonishing thought that the Son of God should develop in Mary's womb from a single-celled zygote to a fully formed baby in just the same way that we all do.

Elizabeth herself immediately knows that Mary has conceived none other than the Son of God, whom Elizabeth calls 'my Lord'. She knows that Mary's baby is the one whose sandal-thong her own son will be unfit to tie. It seems to me that there is something like female intuition going on here, and that it is a reliable form of knowledge. Elizabeth's husband, Zechariah, is the one who received the angelic annunciation that his barren wife would conceive, but he was struck dumb because he didn't believe the message. I know I could be shot down in flames in this day and age for pointing to differences between the sexes. Nevertheless, maybe Zechariah is the over-rationalising male who, as a priest, is well aware of the waiting and longing of his people, but fails to believe, and Elizabeth is the intuiting female who can see the bigger picture and slot it all into place, and who—filled with the Holy Spirit—really does believe.

Mary's poetic response to Elizabeth is known as the Magnificat and has been the subject of innumerable musical settings. This wonderful song of praise sets out beautifully how God's priorities are in direct contrast to our human values. The gospel upsets all our preconceived notions of what and who is important. God blesses Mary herself, his lowly handmaiden. He turns our human hierarchies upside down, toppling the powerful from their thrones and lifting up the lowly. We may take pride in our success, our achievements, our rise to the top of the social ladder, our wealth—but God scatters the proud in the thoughts of their hearts; he fills the hungry with good things, and sends the rich away empty. Yet again, we have the fulfilment of prophecy, the end of longing and waiting: the time to believe is here. This time it is God's promise to the patriarch Abraham that is mentioned (v. 55), which we considered at the beginning of our Advent journey, that through his seed—the son of promise, Isaac, the son of his old age—all the families of the earth will be blessed.

Whenever we think we have achieved something, rather than being proud, let's humble ourselves like Mary. Above all, let's praise God, acknowledging that it is he who blesses our endeavours if we submit to him and believe in his promises, and that only in submitting to his will shall we gain the lasting reward, the crown of life.

For reflection

Magnificat

My soul magnifies the poor
the sore
the raw
and my spirit rejoices in God
my downcast
my outcast
my twig-bone wrongcaste
for he regards the low estate
the no-go estate
the empty plate
and squats there with those generations

For at whose name the Cosmos shakes
and canyons quake
sought sanctuary within a womb
a young girl's chaste, unopened room
a sparse, unblemished catacomb
and holy is he amongst the lame

His mercy is on those who fear him
hear him
those near him
in desert flapping bivouac or dehydrated barrio

The night sky rolled out by his arm,
the preening proud ignore his balm
and slink towards the warlock charm
of their small ambitions
and those on thrones end up alone
replaced by fly-pecked innocents

He only eats with the hungry
and if they don't, he too refrains;
and as for the rich—
a table can not be found for them

My soul magnifies the poor
the sore
the raw
and my spirit rejoices in God
my outcast

STEWART HENDERSON [26]

Our Advent waiting and longing come to fulfilment today as we light the final candle on our Advent wreath. Having lit the four red candles for the patriarchs, prophets, John the Baptist and Mary, now we light the final white candle for Christ himself, 'the light of the world'.

In the wonderful Christmas Eve Service of Nine Lessons and Carols from the Chapel of King's College, Cambridge, this Christmas Gospel reading is announced with the words, 'St John unfolds the great mystery of the incarnation'. And so he does. Matthew and Luke give us the narratives of Jesus' birth. Of course they also give some explanation, especially in the angelic messages, of what is happening, but John, probably writing at the end of the first century, gives no narrative. Instead he reflects on all that has happened since Christ's birth, including his resurrection and the Church's expansion in the power of the Holy Spirit. Hence he writes the deepest theological explanation of all about what has happened—and it is truly staggering.

John's profoundly theological account of the incarnation reminds me in some ways of how science works by piecing together separate pieces of evidence and unifying them in an overarching theory. For example, James Clerk Maxwell, in the 19th century, united the phenomena of electricity and magnetism into a unified theory of electromagnetism. From his theory all the diverse phenomena follow as logical consequences. In a somewhat similar way, John does not need to repeat the well-known nativity stories. Instead he gives an explanation of who Jesus is, which shows why his birth might have been very unusual—why it might have been heralded by angels, and even why a virginal conception would be appropriate.

The opening words, 'In the beginning', take us right back to the first words in our Bibles. In Genesis 1 God spoke creation into being, and now we learn that his Word is a person who was both with God and was God. This is the eternally pre-existent divine Word, the agent of creation. Greek readers of the Gospel would have identified this Word (Greek: *logos*) with the rational principle of order behind the universe.

It is utterly astonishing that a first-century monotheistic Jew could write in these terms, especially when later we read that this pre-existent Word, coexisting in the beginning with God, and being God himself, becomes flesh. The only way the Church could resolve the tension here between mono-theism and Jesus' divinity was through the doctrine of the Trinity, promulgated at the Council of Nicea in AD325—that we believe in one God who is 'Father, Son and Holy Spirit'. This isn't some philosophical abstraction of no importance for our daily lives; it is essential for our salvation. It is because God became human in Jesus Christ that we can become both the true humans we are meant to be and 'participants in the divine nature' (2 Peter 1:4)—surely a mind-blowing thought.

A theme running through John's Gospel, beginning with verse 4 here, is light (described in physics, incidentally, by Maxwell's equations). As God said at the creation, 'Let there be light' (Genesis 1:3), so Jesus proclaims, 'I am the light of the world' (John 8:12). In the villages where I was a curate, there was no street lighting. This was marvellous for star-gazing, but a real problem for anyone wanting to get about after dark. I remember visiting an old lady one winter's evening, stumbling through puddles, tripping and getting wet, and having great difficulty in unlatching the gate to approach her house. I needed a light to guide me in the darkness, but had forgotten my torch. We all need a light to lighten the path before us in life. We need light in our daily lives to enable us to flourish, to become true humans.

The light shining into our hearts may be an uncomfortable spotlight at times, when it reveals some of the uglier things within. That is why some shun the light ('people loved darkness rather than light because their deeds were evil', John 3:19). But how much better it is for our blemishes to be illuminated so that they can be removed. When that is done, we can shine as lights in the world ourselves, reflecting back the light of Christ within us.[29]

Tragically, the creator of the world was rejected. The first and greatest of all Christmas gifts was spurned. People did indeed shun the light. Even 'his own people' did not accept him, but the extraordinary thing is that 'to all who received him, who believed in his name, he gave power to become children of God' (vv. 11–12). As we receive our Christmas gifts today, let us reflect again on that greatest of all gifts, God in human flesh, and on what an amazing privilege it is to be a Christian—to partake in the divine nature, to be fully alive, to be lit up and reflect the glory of God, to be a child of God. Isn't it sometimes overwhelming to realise all these riches we have in Christ?

For reflection

Moonless darkness stands between.
Past, O Past, no more be seen!
But the Bethlehem star may lead me
To the sight of Him who freed me
From the self that I have been.

Make me pure, Lord: Thou art holy;
Make me meek, Lord: Thou wert lowly;
Now beginning, and alway:
Now begin, on Christmas day.

GERARD MANLEY HOPKINS

The cost of believing

No sooner have we rejoiced in the coming of the Saviour than we are reminded of what it costs to follow him. We commemorate Stephen, the first of countless Christian martyrs. In a world where children are abused and exploited on an industrial scale, we remember Herod's slaughter of the innocents. The world was the same then as now, and this is the world that Christ entered in order to redeem it. We must walk in the light in a world enveloped in darkness. We must take up the cross knowing that this is a world in which evil abounds, but that he has overcome the world.

26 DECEMBER (ST STEPHEN'S DAY)

Martyrdom

'You stiff-necked people, uncircumcised in heart and ears, you are for ever opposing the Holy Spirit, just as your ancestors used to do. Which of the prophets did your ancestors not persecute? They killed those who foretold the coming of the Righteous One, and now you have become his betrayers and murderers. You are the ones that received the law as ordained by angels, and yet you have not kept it.'

When they heard these things, they became enraged and ground their teeth at Stephen. But filled with the Holy Spirit, he gazed into heaven and saw the glory of God and Jesus standing at the right hand of God. 'Look,' he said, 'I see the heavens opened and the Son of Man standing at the right hand of God!' But they covered their ears, and with a loud shout all rushed together against him. Then they dragged him out of the city and began to stone him; and the witnesses laid their coats at the feet of a young man named Saul. While they were stoning Stephen, he prayed, 'Lord Jesus, receive my spirit.' Then he knelt down and cried out in a loud voice, 'Lord, do not hold this sin against them.' When he had said this, he died.

ACTS 7: 51–60

The longing and waiting of men and women down the ages is over; the Messiah has come, but this is the beginning of the story, not the end. We continue to wait, as we have been reminding ourselves from 1 December, for his second coming in glory. Believing that he will indeed bring the whole space–time universe to its magnificent consummation, we now explore what it means to live in the 'now and not yet'.

Although the majority of us will no longer distribute gift boxes to our servants today, we still generally refer to it as Boxing Day, and it still has its own customs, such as a Boxing Day hunt in many parts of the country. The church, however, pulls us up fast in the midst of our festivities, for today we commemorate the first martyr, St Stephen. Indeed, the three days immediately following Christmas Day are all important festivals. Believing that the long-awaited Messiah has come, we now focus on the cost of following him and making him known in the world he came to save.

Stephen was one of a group of seven deacons appointed by the apostles to distribute food (Acts 6). He was a man 'full of faith and the Holy Spirit' (v. 5), necessary qualities for what, in the world's eyes, would be a menial role. For Stephen, waiting at tables, care for the poor, working signs and wonders and exercising wisdom in disputation with opponents were all of a piece.

Stephen paid the ultimate price for his discipleship, dying a brutal death. In his sermon just before he died, he pointed to the way that past generations had treated the prophets and how the present generation had betrayed their own Messiah, the Righteous One. Stephen's heavenly vision recalls Jesus' own words before Caiaphas, 'From now on you will see the Son of Man seated at the right hand of Power and coming on the clouds of heaven' (Matthew 26:64). Perhaps the very familiarity of those words, so recently spoken by Jesus, was what enraged the Council against Stephen.

We are living today in an age of unprecedented persecution of Christians. Many of our brothers and sisters around the world are experiencing violence, imprisonment and martyrdom because they are disciples of Jesus Christ. As I write, there is news of churches being attacked and Christians killed, imprisoned or fleeing for their lives in Nigeria, Egypt, Sudan and Pakistan, to name but four countries. In Tanzania, in a typical example of such persecution, a new church was being inaugurated when a bomb was thrown into it, killing five worshippers inside. In Peshawar, Pakistan, 127 people have been killed in an attack on a church.

In some countries it is illegal to build churches, and conversion to Christianity can be at pain of death. Hundreds of thousands of Christians have fled Iraq in the face of persecution in the years following the invasion by Britain and the US in 2003. Many of these believers went to Syria and, as I write, are now fleeing again. Quite recently two bishops, and, some time afterwards, twelve nuns were kidnapped in Syria. Iraq and Syria have some of the earliest Christian communities still existing, some even speaking Aramaic, the language of Jesus, yet they are being persecuted to the point of extinction.

Dietrich Bonhoeffer was executed by Hitler because he resisted the Nazi régime in Germany. He is one of ten 20th-century Christian martyrs commemorated in niches over the west door of Westminster Abbey. In his book, *The Cost of Discipleship* (1937), he describes what it really means to 'take up the cross'. 'When Christ calls a man, he bids him come and die,' he says, and he goes on, 'Discipleship means allegiance to the suffering Christ, and it is therefore not at all surprising that Christians should be called upon to suffer. In fact it is a joy and a token of his grace.' [30]

Bonhoeffer writes that the early Christian martyrs were

assured of the joy of Christ's presence at the hour of their agony. These are hard words but they describe what Stephen experienced and what Bonhoeffer himself came to experience when he was hanged. Tertullian, in the second century, said that 'the blood of the martyrs is the seed of the Church'. That was true then and it is still true today, but it is a hard lesson.

There have been some worrying cases of the rights of Christians being infringed in Britain in recent years. We are increasingly being told that our religion is a private matter. Some Christians have even been told that they should take up another job if they are unwilling to follow some newly introduced practice that contradicts their beliefs. Yet our experiences pale beside those of our brothers and sisters elsewhere in the world. Can we identify with their plight? Can we take up the cross for our suffering brothers and sisters, making their case, praying for them and contributing to the relief of their suffering?

In the midst of our festivities, can we, who have it so easy, spare some thoughts and prayers for those suffering today for their faith in the child of Bethlehem?

For prayer

Gracious Father, who gave the first martyr Stephen grace to pray for those who took up stones against him: grant that in all our sufferings for the truth we may learn to love even our enemies and to seek forgiveness for those who desire our hurt, looking up to heaven to him who was crucified for us, Jesus Christ, our mediator and advocate, who is alive and reigns with you, in the unity of the Holy Spirit, one God, now and for ever. Amen

COLLECT FOR ST STEPHEN, *COMMON WORSHIP*

Walking in the light

We declare to you what was from the beginning, what we have heard, what we have seen with our eyes, what we have looked at and touched with our hands, concerning the word of life—this life was revealed, and we have seen it and testify to it, and declare to you the eternal life that was with the Father and was revealed to us—we declare to you what we have seen and heard so that you also may have fellowship with us; and truly our fellowship is with the Father and with his Son Jesus Christ. We are writing these things so that our joy may be complete.

This is the message we have heard from him and proclaim to you, that God is light and in him there is no darkness at all. If we say that we have fellowship with him while we are walking in darkness, we lie and do not do what is true; but if we walk in the light as he himself is in the light, we have fellowship with one another, and the blood of Jesus his Son cleanses us from all sin. If we say that we have no sin, we deceive ourselves, and the truth is not in us. If we confess our sins, he who is faithful and just will forgive us our sins and cleanse us from all unrighteousness. If we say that we have not sinned, we make him a liar, and his word is not in us.

1 JOHN 1:1–10

Today we celebrate John the Evangelist by reading from the first of the three epistles that bear his name. The author is traditionally identified with the 'beloved disciple' in John's Gospel. As Richard Bauckham says, there is little reason to doubt the beloved disciple's own testimony that he wrote the Gospel (John 21:24). Bauckham convincingly argues that, in the first five verses of today's passage, the 'we' is a substitute for 'I', used for authoritative personal testimony. It is a bit like the English royal 'we' or authorial 'we'.[31]

The opening of today's passage bears significant resemblance to the opening of John's Gospel. The writer tells us that he is giving eyewitness testimony to Jesus as a physical, flesh-and-blood reality. Jesus embodies in his person eternal life, and yet he walked the earth as a human being who could be seen and touched. He could also be seen and touched after his resurrection. Indeed, Jesus invited doubting Thomas to see and touch him (John 20:27), although, in the event, Thomas apparently did not do so.

John couldn't make it clearer that he is witness to a real, factual, physical experience of hearing Jesus' words and seeing what he did, including rising from the dead. He is writing his letter because he wants his readers to share in the same fellowship that he experiences with God the Father and his Son Jesus Christ. John's Gospel is equally clear: for example, in John 20:30–31 we read, 'Now Jesus did many other signs in the presence of his disciples, which are not written in this book. But these are written so that you may come to believe that Jesus is the Messiah, the Son of God, and that through believing you may have life in his name.'

John is proclaiming eternal life in Christ, and he tells us clearly what this eternal life is (John 17:3): 'And this is eternal life, that they may know you, the only true God, and

Jesus Christ whom you have sent.' We are assured that this knowledge of God and Jesus Christ, which begins now, will go on for ever because of the resurrection.

Sometimes it's said that the only true form of knowledge is that given by science, based on repeatable experiments. A moment's reflection will tell us that that cannot be true. There are many things I know in ways that are not scientific. For example, I know from memory that I had corn-flakes for breakfast yesterday. I know that it is morally wrong to murder or steal. (What experiment could possibly show that?) I know that King Henry VIII had six wives, because we have the reliable testimony of contemporaries and the writings of historians. In fact, we believe a lot of things on the basis of the testimony of reliable witnesses. This is the equivalent in history of experimental evidence for a hypothesis in science, and can be used in a similar manner to substantiate a historical hypothesis.

The former Professor of Philosophy of Religion at Oxford, Richard Swinburne, has formulated two important principles, the 'principle of credulity' and the 'principle of testimony'. The 'principle of credulity' states that, under normal circumstances (that is, excluding such factors as my having taken hallucinatory drugs), I should believe my own experiences. The 'principle of testimony' states that, again under normal circumstances, I should believe the testimony of reliable witnesses—even witnesses to unusual events, such as miracles. We might need to investigate how reliable the witnesses are, and whether the circumstances were abnormal in some way, but usually we should accept people's testimony, just as John is asking us to do.

In the second part of today's passage, John tells his readers what the message of Jesus is, namely that 'God is light and in him is no darkness at all' (v. 5). In John's Gospel, too, there is much about light: 'The true light, which enlightens everyone, was coming into the world' (1:9); 'I am the light of the world. Whoever follows me will never walk in darkness but will have the light of life' (8:12). Sadly, however, 'people loved darkness rather than light because their deeds were evil' (3:19).

The contrast between light and darkness is therefore a moral one. To walk in the light is to live according to the truth. To become a Christian is to move from the kingdom of darkness into the kingdom of light.

To walk in the light is to be righteous, to do good, to love God and to love our neighbour as ourselves, but of course we all fail. We let God down. We don't love him and our neighbour as we should. In short, we sin, and it is self-deception to deny that we sin. The good news, as 1 John 1:9 reminds us, is that 'if we confess our sins, he who is faithful and just will forgive us our sins and cleanse us from all unrighteousness'.

It isn't always easy to love. No doubt we find some people especially difficult to love. We need to ask God to forgive us and help us to love even those people who really annoy us, and even those who deliberately cause us harm. This is what it means to 'walk in the light', and this is what will last into eternity. Hatred and falsehood, the things of darkness, will cease to exist, but if we walk in the light we shall enjoy fellowship with God the Father and his Son Jesus Christ for ever.

For reflection

Think of someone you find difficult to love and hold them before God as you ask him these questions:

- *What it is about me that makes me negative towards this other person?*
- *Does he/she reflect some character trait or behaviour that I dislike in myself?*
- *Does he/she invade what I consider to be 'my precious time' and 'my busy life'?*
- *Do I think I am more important to God than he/she is?*

Imagine both of you sitting with Jesus, in the light of his love, and listen to what he says.

28 DECEMBER
(HOLY INNOCENTS)

Dark deeds

Now after they had left, an angel of the Lord appeared to Joseph in a dream and said, 'Get up, take the child and his mother, and flee to Egypt, and remain there until I tell you; for Herod is about to search for the child, to destroy him.' Then Joseph got up, took the child and his mother by night, and went to Egypt, and remained there until the death of Herod. This was to fulfil what had been spoken by the Lord through the prophet, 'Out of Egypt I have called my son.'

When Herod saw that he had been tricked by the wise men, he was infuriated, and he sent and killed all the children in and around Bethlehem who were two years old or under, according to the time that he had learned from the wise men. Then was fulfilled what had been spoken through the prophet Jeremiah:

'A voice was heard in Ramah,
wailing and loud lamentation,
Rachel weeping for her children;
she refused to be consoled, because they are no more.'
MATTHEW 2:13–18

My scientific mindset prompts me to ask, what evidence do we have about Herod? The Herod featured here is known as 'Herod the Great'. There is no historical record outside scripture to support this account of the massacre of children, but it is entirely in keeping with what we know of Herod's character. Herod was a brute who killed two of his own sons because he thought they were plotting against him. He was a megalomaniac who built a number of fortresses in and around Judea. The slaughter of a few children would hardly rank as worthy of comment in the reign of such a character.

Herod was put on the throne by the Romans and ruled from 37 to 4BC (which, incidentally, means that Jesus must have been born in 4BC at the latest). Josephus acknowledges some benefits bestowed by Herod but also says this:

When anyone looks upon the punishments he inflicted, and the injuries he did not only to his subjects, but to his nearest relations, and takes notice of his severe and unrelenting disposition there, he will be forced to allow that he was brutish, and a stranger to all humanity.[32]

Matthew's account of the slaughter of the children reminds us powerfully of the story of Moses in the Old Testament. Just as Pharaoh killed all the children under two years of age, so Herod does the same. Moses was hidden in a basket in the bulrushes and was rescued by Pharaoh's daughter; Jesus was taken by Mary and Joseph into Egypt to escape Herod. As God called his son (meaning the people of Israel, Hosea 11:1) out of Egypt, so God's Son, Jesus, returns with Mary and Joseph to settle in Nazareth. For Matthew, Jesus is the new, much greater Moses, leading people out of their slavery to sin and bringing into being the 'new Israel' in which God's law is written on people's hearts.

In the midst of our festivities, the story of the Holy Innocents reminds us, like the story of Stephen, of the reality of human brutality and of despotic rulers in particular. It reminds us of the suffering we inflict on each other as humans, which Christ came to submit to and, thereby, defeat.

The 20th century witnessed human brutality on an unprecedented scale, so it is very surprising that today's atheists should blame religion as the cause of all or most wars. Despotic anti-religious tyrants like Hitler, Stalin, Pol Pot, Mao Zedong, and their régimes, committed appalling atrocities, and, sadly, modern science was used in aid of such cruelty. As Winston Churchill put it in June 1940:

If we fail, then the whole world, including the United States, including all that we have known and cared for, will sink into the abyss of a new Dark Age, made more sinister, and perhaps more protracted, by the lights of perverted science.[33]

As a scientist, I am aware of the great benefits that science has brought to humankind but also the ways in which science has been perverted in the service of the baser human tendencies. As the theory that explains the origin of species and our own evolution from other animals, Darwinism is ethically neutral, but if it is turned into a social philosophy (advocating that societies should weed out the 'weak', the 'imbecile' or the 'inferior race') then we end up with eugenics and, ultimately, the gas chambers.

One of the remarkable achievements of Rowan Williams during his time as Archbishop of Canterbury was to produce a brilliant book on the 19th-century Russian author Fyodor Dostoevsky.[34] A significant point that emerges from Williams' book is how, contrary to what the new atheists tell us, without God there can be no basis for morality. If the source of morality is simply the human will, then there are no grounds for asserting the unique value of every human person. An abstract view of human happiness results, which is prepared to engage in mass slaughter for the supposed general good.

Today's world still contains cruel despots, as well as refugees who flee their régimes. It is fundamentally the same world that Jesus entered, and he came into the heart of its worst excesses. Like many people today, the holy family became refugees in a foreign land. Not only did God become one of us, but he loved us so much that, for our sake, he became a victim of the most terrible human brutality. Only so could he bring his people out of slavery as Moses did of old. As we pray for those caught up in all manner of suffering today, let us remember that our Lord Jesus submitted himself to just such horrors and defeated all evil on the cross—and therein lies our hope.

For prayer

Gracious Lord, we cry out to you for children who are victims of crime and aggression, especially those who are refugees and orphans as a result of civil wars across the world. We pray that all needy children may find food, shelter, support and love through the care and compassion of Christ-like adults and aid workers. For your love's sake. Amen

Do not be afraid

'A disciple is not above the teacher, nor a slave above the master; it is enough for the disciple to be like the teacher, and the slave like the master. If they have called the master of the house Beelzebul, how much more will they malign those of his household!

'So have no fear of them; for nothing is covered up that will not be uncovered, and nothing secret that will not become known. What I say to you in the dark, tell in the light; and what you hear whispered, proclaim from the housetops. Do not fear those who kill the body but cannot kill the soul; rather fear him who can destroy both soul and body in hell. Are not two sparrows sold for a penny? Yet not one of them will fall to the ground unperceived by your Father. And even the hairs of your head are all counted. So do not be afraid; you are of more value than many sparrows.

'Everyone therefore who acknowledges me before others, I also will acknowledge before my Father in heaven; but whoever denies me before others, I also will deny before my Father in heaven.'

MATTHEW 10:24–33

Today we celebrate St Thomas Becket, the Archbishop of Canterbury who was murdered in his own cathedral because he stood up for the rights of the church against King Henry II. As we saw on St Stephen's Day, we don't have to go back to the twelfth century to find examples of martyrdom, since there are all too many martyrs in our own day and age. In Matthew 10, Jesus tells us that this is just what his disciples are to expect when they preach the good news of God's kingdom and live out its values by bringing wholeness and healing to shattered lives. They will be hated for it; they will be persecuted and brought before tribunals for it.

What is our reaction when we face opposition because of our faith? Do we cave in under pressure? Do we say, 'Enough is enough; anything for a quiet life' and give up preaching Christ? Do we give up on bringing his compassion and healing to a needy world? On the contrary, says Jesus, we are to proclaim his message 'from the housetops' (v. 27). Jesus tells us not to fear. One day, the secrets of all hearts will be disclosed. Justice will be done in the end and we shall be vindicated.

We are not to fear any human being, for human power, however evil, is limited. A human being can only kill the body, but our life is more than our body, more than the sum total of our physical parts. To kill the body is not to kill the soul, the person that we are. Only God can destroy both body and soul in Gehenna (see 3 January), and therefore it is God alone whom we are to fear. This present body is just the perishable seed (1 Corinthians 15:42) and the perishable must put on the imperishable (v. 53).

The power that humans possess is limited, and they possess it only because God has given it to them. Pilate asked Jesus, 'Do you not know that I have power to release you, and power to crucify you?' but Jesus answered, 'You would have no power over me unless it were given you from above'

(John 19:10–11). It is a sign of God's great love for humans that he has created us with the tremendous freedom we have. God desires us to exercise this freedom responsibly, with love and compassion for our fellows, but, sadly, we all too often abuse that freedom.

God's power is of a different order. He created the universe out of nothing, and all that exists does so because he wills it to exist and because he upholds it in being. As we saw when considering the family saga of Joseph, God has the power to bring about his purposes in the world despite humans' evil intentions. God also has the power to recreate, to make new, to renew the creation. Only God has power to raise from the dead: he has exercised that power mightily in raising Christ and will exercise it again in raising us. Bonhoeffer even said, paradoxically, that by his resurrection we know about the creation, reversing the order of our knowledge about God.[35] Because our God is this God, with this power, we have no need to fear.

We are assured that God cares for us intimately. No sparrow falls to the ground apart from his will, but we are worth far more than many sparrows. God's concern for us is so detailed that he counts even the hairs of our head. This does not mean that we shall escape suffering and persecution in this life on account of our following Christ. No, as Bonhoeffer says, to be a Christian is to 'watch with Christ in Gethsemane' and to 'share in God's sufferings'.[36] It does not, therefore, mean an easy life, but it does mean that Jesus will be with us in our sufferings and that Jesus will acknowledge us before his father in heaven (Matthew 10:32). Thus our eternal destiny is secure. Our names are written in the Lamb's book of life (Revelation 21:27), and that is what ultimately matters.

Are we fearful of other human beings? In Britain we are

more likely to be mocked for our faith than killed for it. Mockery is unpleasant, but worse things can happen, such as a care worker being disciplined for offering to pray for a client. This seems quite bizarre in a country in which it is still a legal requirement that prayers be said every day in our schools, and in which Parliament begins its sessions with prayers said by bishops who, by our constitution, sit in the House of Lords. Paradox abounds, but the secularist agenda is gaining ground. The question is, do we have the courage still to proclaim Christ and bring wholeness and healing to people's lives in his name? The rational, scientific side of me says that of course I must always stand up for Jesus and his values. However, 'the spirit indeed is willing, but the flesh is weak' (Mark 14:38).

Earlier in Matthew 10, Jesus tells us to rely on the Holy Spirit for what to say when confronted by persecution (vv. 19–20). If we try to serve Christ in our own strength, we are very likely to fail, so let us pray daily for the Spirit's empowering in all the circumstances we are going to meet, and let us pray for his help to keep in mind the eternal perspective.

For prayer

Pray for strength and courage for those experiencing persecution, and for the peace that only God can bring. Thank God that his grace is sufficient for their needs (2 Corinthians 12:9). Pray that their faith will not fail, but that their suffering will draw them closer to him and increase their faith. Pray too that the Holy Spirit will enable persecuted Christians to forgive and love their persecutors (Matthew 5:44) and that their Christ-like reactions will have an impact on their persecutors.[37]

Living in the 'now and not yet'

Christ has come and he will come again. We have to live with sin and death in the inbetween time, yet we can do so because Christ has risen victorious over sin and death, which are mortally wounded forces. Christ's victory is good news for all people, regardless of race, gender or social status, but are we equipped to take this message of his great love and compassion, his forgiveness and mercy into the world? The answer is yes, because we have been given powerful resources and have confidence that our inheritance is secure. We are children of Abraham, blessed by his seed, just as God promised. So we journey on in the hope and expectation of reaching our eternal home, the new Jerusalem, which will come as a bride adorned for her husband.

Feeding on Christ

Jesus said to them, 'I am the bread of life. Whoever comes to me will never be hungry, and whoever believes in me will never be thirsty. But I said to you that you have seen me and yet do not believe. Everything that the Father gives me will come to me, and anyone who comes to me I will never drive away; for I have come down from heaven, not to do my own will, but the will of him who sent me. And this is the will of him who sent me, that I should lose nothing of all that he has given me, but raise it up on the last day. This is indeed the will of my Father, that all who see the Son and believe in him may have eternal life; and I will raise them up on the last day.'

Then the Jews began to complain about him because he said, 'I am the bread that came down from heaven.' They were saying, 'Is not this Jesus, the son of Joseph, whose father and mother we know? How can he now say, "I have come down from heaven"?' Jesus answered them, 'Do not complain among yourselves. No one can come to me unless drawn by the Father who sent me; and I will raise that person up on the last day. It is written in the prophets, "And they shall all be taught by God." Everyone who has heard and learned from the Father comes to me. Not that anyone has seen the Father except the one who is from God; he has seen the Father. Very truly, I tell you, whoever believes has eternal life. I am the bread of life. Your ancestors ate the manna in the wilderness, and they died. This is the bread that comes down from heaven, so that one may eat of it and not die. I am the living bread that came down from heaven. Whoever eats of this bread will live for ever; and the bread that I will give for the life of the world is my flesh.'

JOHN 6:35–51

Jesus has come and we have, I trust, been celebrating his coming among us 'in great humility', as we set out to do at the beginning of our Advent journey. That much longing and waiting is over. Jesus has come and, by his coming, has won the victory over sin and death on the cross and risen triumphantly from the dead. But we have to continue in the here and now as we long and wait, believing that he will come again 'in glory to judge the quick and the dead' (in the words of the creed). During this period of what theologians call 'inaugurated eschatology'—the time of 'already and not yet'—we are, of course, not alone. Christ has sent the Holy Spirit to indwell us, teach and guide us, even to pray on our behalf (Romans 8:26). Jesus comes to us in the Eucharist— indeed, an important aspect of the Spirit's activity as we ask, in the Prayer of Consecration, that 'by the power of the Holy Spirit these gifts of bread and wine may be to us his body and his blood'. Here we are reminded of Christ's sacrifice on the cross, the benefits of which are made present for us as we obey Jesus' command, 'Take, eat; this is my body. Do this in remembrance of me.'

John's Gospel contains no account of the institution of the Eucharist, whereas Matthew, Mark and Luke all do. Even though so great a theologian as Martin Luther thought that John 6 was not about the Eucharist, it seems to many modern commentators that, on the contrary, it is a profound reflection on the Eucharist.

Jesus' self-description as the 'bread of life' comes immediately after the feeding of the 5000. The timing is significant, coinciding with the feast of the Passover. This festival reminded the Jews of their deliverance from slavery in Egypt, followed by their journeyings in the wilderness for 40 years, their being fed by manna from heaven, the receipt of the law by Moses on Mount Sinai, and their entry into the promised land. As God had fed the Israelites in the wilderness, so he fed Elijah on his journey to the same mountain, and so Jesus feeds 5000 from a boy's offering of five barley loaves and two fish. This is an acted parable. The ultimate food, the real bread from heaven, Jesus tells us, is his very self.

When we eat physical food, we always get hungry again. Jesus says that those who come to him will never hunger or thirst. How do we come to him and receive him? The wonderful thing is that our coming to him is his own gift to us, not something we can earn or achieve by our own effort, as we saw on 20 December. That is the meaning of Jesus' words, 'No one can come to me unless drawn by the Father who sent me'; he goes on to say, 'and I will raise that person up at the last day' (v. 44). He says that whoever feeds on him, the living bread, will live for ever (v. 51). The Israelites who ate the manna in the wilderness died; those who feed on Jesus, the living bread, will not die.

Remarkably, this is why Jesus came into the world: to offer himself as the living bread and to raise us from death to life. Without Jesus, death is the ultimate enemy, the source of despair, the fact we all have to face, which seems to render all human endeavour and achievement meaningless. With Jesus, death is the doorway to eternal life. Yet that gift of eternal life begins now. Our physical death is not the end of us. Life continues beyond the grave into full and complete communion with God and with all of redeemed humanity.

The Eucharist is the present manifestation and foretaste of all this. As the Communion tells us, we are joined together with Jesus as we 'feed on him in our hearts by faith with thanksgiving'. We are also joined together with our fellow believers, since, 'though we are many, we are one body, because we all share in one bread'. We become part of the body at baptism. We stay united in the body through the communal meal, the Eucharist. So, we are united horizontally with our fellow believers, and united vertically with Christ, whom we encounter as we receive the elements of bread and wine. And this meal, stylised in the liturgy and owing so much to the Jewish Passover, which Jesus was celebrating when instituting it, is a foretaste of the heavenly banquet. Then we shall sit at table with Christ in his eternal kingdom, enjoying uninterrupted and perfected fellowship with him and each other. Maybe a good new year's resolution would be to be more regular in our participation in the Eucharist and so, as Paul exhorts us, 'proclaim the Lord's death until he comes' (1 Corinthians 11:26).

For reflection

Love's choice
This bread is light, dissolving, almost air,
A little visitation on my tongue,
A wafer-thin sensation, hardly there.
This taste of wine is brief in flavour, flung
A moment to the palate's roof and fled,
Even its aftertaste a memory.

Yet this is how He comes. Through wine and bread
Love chooses to be emptied into me.
He does not come in unimagined light
Too bright to be denied, too absolute
For consciousness, too strong for sight,
Leaving the seer blind, the poet mute;
Chooses instead to seep into each sense,
To dye himself into experience.

MALCOLM GUITE, A SONNET FOR CORPUS CHRISTI [38]

31 DECEMBER

Immersed in scripture

Now you have observed my teaching, my conduct, my aim in life, my faith, my patience, my love, my steadfastness, my persecutions, and my suffering the things that happened to me in Antioch, Iconium, and Lystra. What persecutions I endured! Yet the Lord rescued me from all of them. Indeed, all who want to live a godly life in Christ Jesus will be persecuted. But wicked people and impostors will go from bad to worse, deceiving others and being deceived. But as for you, continue in what you have learned and firmly believed, knowing from whom you learned it, and how from childhood you have known the sacred writings that are able to instruct you for salvation through faith in Christ Jesus. All scripture is inspired by God and is useful for teaching, for reproof, for correction, and for training in righteousness, so that everyone who belongs to God may be proficient, equipped for every good work.

2 TIMOTHY 3:10–17

Today we commemorate John Wycliffe, who was ahead of his time in advocating reform of the church in the 14th century. He brought a renewed emphasis on the Bible as the source of doctrine and criticised church practices and doctrines that were not founded on scripture. Disciples of Wycliffe, inspired by their teacher, translated the Bible into English.

Today's passage points up the supreme importance of holy scripture. Paul reminds his disciple Timothy of his (Paul's) own life of faith, including his persecutions. Just like Jesus, Paul says that the godly are to expect to be persecuted. On the other hand, he points out that 'wicked people and imposters will go from bad to worse, deceiving others and being deceived' (v. 13). So how are we to avoid false teaching? The only way is to be immersed in the scriptures, as Timothy had been since childhood. We read at the beginning of this letter how Paul saw that Timothy's faith had been fostered by his grandmother Lois and mother Eunice. These devout women, like Augustine's mother Monica, were responsible for the faith of one of the great figures of the early church.

Timothy was entrusted by Paul to establish the Thessalonians in their faith and encourage them in their afflictions (1 Thessalonians 3:2–3). Paul also sent him to Corinth with the same message as in today's passage: to imitate Paul and not be deceived by false teachers, and not to go beyond what is written (1 Corinthians 4:6, 16–17). Furthermore, in his first letter to Timothy, Paul had urged him to remain at Ephesus to counter false teachers (1 Timothy 1:3). It seems that Timothy did just that, because the church historian Eusebius tells us that Timothy was the first bishop of Ephesus, and there is some evidence that he was martyred under the Emperor Domitian.

Paul tells Timothy that 'the sacred writings', or scriptures, 'are able to instruct you [literally 'make you wise', as in KJV] for salvation through faith in Christ Jesus' (v. 15). Article 6 of the Church of England's 39 articles of religion captures what Paul is saying here very well:

Holy Scripture containeth all things necessary to salvation: so that whatsoever is not read therein, nor may be proved thereby, is not to be required of any man, that it should be believed as an article of the Faith, or be thought requisite or necessary for salvation.

In other words, the Bible contains everything you need to be saved. If you don't find an idea there, or cannot back up your belief from scripture, then you don't need that idea or belief in order to be a Christian.

Paul goes on to say that 'all scripture is inspired by God' (v. 16), which, at the time, would have meant the scriptures of the Old Testament. It is impossible to understand the New Testament without the Old. Unless we read the Old Testament, we cannot see God's plan for humankind worked out in the history of his people, the Jews. Jesus is the Jewish Messiah. He is the prophet like Moses whom God was to raise up (Deuteronomy 18:15). Jesus is the king in the line of David who was to rule God's peaceable kingdom for ever. He is the Son of Man and Son of God in whom the longing, waiting and believing of the patriarchs and prophets have been so wonderfully fulfilled.

Paul lists what scripture is useful for—teaching, reproof, correction and training in righteousness—and, because Christians often get the wrong end of the stick, it is worth noting what he does not say. The Bible is not a scientific text book; it is not a treatise on cosmology or biology. As John Calvin said, 'He who would learn astronomy and other recondite arts, let him go elsewhere.' Science is of immense value, a great gift from God when we consider all the benefits it has brought. The fact that we can do science is a consequence of our being made in the image of God. But scripture is profitable for far more important things than science. Scripture teaches us about our eternal destiny and the free grace of God in Christ that brings it about. Scripture admonishes us and guides us into the right path when we do wrong or are in error. It 'trains us in righteousness'. Thus it enables the Christian to be 'proficient, equipped for every good work' (v. 17).

What a great debt we owe to John Wycliffe and those he inspired to give the Bible to every one of us in our own language! Its riches are no longer the preserve of an élite trained in ancient tongues. When we consider that successors of Wycliffe such as William Tyndale, burned at the stake in 1536 for the 'heresy' of translating the Bible, have given their lives for doing us this great service, how can we not immerse ourselves in the scriptures, as Paul and Timothy did, and let them shape us into the people God means us to be?

For reflection and prayer

Think about the following questions.

- *Am I immersing myself in scripture?*
- *If not, can I begin daily reading, perhaps using BRF notes?*
- *Can I buy some modern commentaries and deepen my understanding of God's word?*

Close by praying the Collect for Bible Sunday:

Blessed Lord, who caused all holy Scriptures to be written for our learning: help us so to hear them, to read, mark, learn and inwardly digest them, that through patience, and the comfort of your holy word, we may embrace and for ever hold fast the hope of everlasting life, which you have given us in our Saviour Jesus Christ, who is alive and reigns with you, in the unity of the Holy Spirit, one God, now and for ever. Amen.[39]

1 JANUARY (THE NAMING AND CIRCUMCISION OF CHRIST)

Children of Abraham

When the angels had left them and gone into heaven, the shepherds said to one another, 'Let us go now to Bethlehem and see this thing that has taken place, which the Lord has made known to us.' So they went with haste and found Mary and Joseph, and the child lying in the manger. When they saw this, they made known what had been told them about this child; and all who heard it were amazed at what the shepherds told them. But Mary treasured all these words and pondered them in her heart. The shepherds returned, glorifying and praising God for all they had heard and seen, as it had been told them.

After eight days had passed, it was time to circumcise the child; and he was called Jesus, the name given by the angel before he was conceived in the womb.

LUKE 2:15–21

Our passage today picks up the nativity story at the point when the shepherds dash off to see what the angels have been talking about. They do indeed see Mary and Joseph and the babe lying in a manger. It is surely no accident that the first visitors to the one who is to be the shepherd of Israel are themselves shepherds. Jesus inherits the throne of his father David, who was taken from the flocks to become king. How right it is that the prophesied shepherd-king should be born in David's city, Bethlehem!

It is also not surprising that the shepherds cannot keep to themselves what they have heard and that their story causes amazement when they tell it. As they return to their flocks, their joy is uncontainable, so they go on their way glorifying and praising God. Mary, however, quietly ponders these things in her heart. She no doubt reflects on how it all fits in with the words of her own angelic visitor, and surely she will go on reflecting on the meaning of it throughout her life.

I hope and pray that, as we have travelled once again, in our imagination, to Bethlehem, we have been captivated afresh by what God has done in and through this child, his only begotten Son. The Lord of sea and sky cradled in his mother's arms! Do we contain our joy or do we, like the shepherds, go on our way glorifying and praising God? Surely there is a lesson here for mission in today's world. Where is God's Spirit at work? Where is Christ being formed in our own community? What can we do with that 'which the Lord has made known to us' (v. 15)? Will we join in the great adventure of forthtelling? Can we, like Mary, take time to ponder in our hearts and discover more and more of the depth and riches of God's dealings with us humans—perhaps through the discipline of contemplative prayer?

Today we celebrate the naming and circumcision of Christ. Mary and Joseph were devout Jews who, like Mary's cousin Elizabeth and her husband Zechariah, had been waiting for God to fulfil his promises. Mary and Joseph therefore did all that was required according to the Jewish law. The baby was named Jesus, meaning 'Yahweh saves', just as the angel Gabriel had said he should be named before he was conceived. And, as was the case from the time of Abraham, the boy was circumcised on the eighth day (Genesis 17:12).

Jesus is thus properly initiated into the covenant people of God. From childhood to adulthood he will be immersed in the Judaism of his day. He will debate in the temple with the teachers of the law when only twelve years old (Luke 2:46–47). He will begin his ministry in the synagogue in Nazareth, reading probably the lectionary lesson of the day and declaring that the prophecy is fulfilled in him (4:16–21). He will be called 'Rabbi', like other Jewish teachers.

Jesus, though, is not just another true Israelite, or even just another first-century rabbi; he is the one who fulfils the whole destiny of the Jewish people—longed for, waited for and believed in through all the trials and tribulations of over 2000 years of history. He is the one, born into a devout and humble family, through whom all the families of the earth will be blessed. He will become the suffering servant who is 'wounded for our transgressions' and 'crushed for our iniquities' (Isaiah 53:5). He will bring his people finally out of exile. He will be the one who judges the world, yet by whose death the sins of the world will be expiated. All that we have been reading over the last few weeks during Advent has been leading up to this birth of this child.

Although a Jew, Jesus brings into being a community in which 'there is no longer Jew or Greek, there is no longer slave nor free, there is no longer male and female' (Galatians 3:28). God's purpose for the world was channelled through this particular people over millennia and focused finally on to this one descendant of Abraham, but the salvation that Jesus brings is for all people: we are all now 'children of Abraham'.

We become members of this new community not by male circumcision but by baptism, whether we are male or female. It is marvellous to reflect on how this community has gone global, from making its first inroads into the known world of the day, mostly incorporated in the Roman Empire, to its spread into the worldwide body of over two billion people that it is today.

Let us ponder the depth and riches of God's dealing with us and go on our way glorifying and praising God.

For reflection

Find a time when you can be on your own. Sit or kneel in the quiet, allowing your body to become still.

Let go of the busyness of the day and breathe slowly and deeply.

Become aware of the sounds around you and, beyond them, of the presence of God, in whom we live and move and have our being.

In the silence, open your heart to God and ponder the depth of his love for his world.

Faithful in prayer and worship

When the time came for their purification according to the law of Moses, they brought him up to Jerusalem to present him to the Lord (as it is written in the law of the Lord, 'Every firstborn male shall be designated as holy to the Lord'), and they offered a sacrifice according to what is stated in the law of the Lord, 'a pair of turtle-doves or two young pigeons.'

Now there was a man in Jerusalem whose name was Simeon; this man was righteous and devout, looking forward to the consolation of Israel, and the Holy Spirit rested on him. It had been revealed to him by the Holy Spirit that he would not see death before he had seen the Lord's Messiah. Guided by the Spirit, Simeon came into the temple; and when the parents brought in the child Jesus, to do for him what was customary under the law, Simeon took him in his arms and praised God, saying,

'Master, now you are dismissing your servant in peace,
according to your word;
for my eyes have seen your salvation
which you have prepared in the presence of all peoples,
a light for revelation to the Gentiles
and for glory to your people Israel.'

And the child's father and mother were amazed at what was being said about him. Then Simeon blessed them and said to his mother Mary, 'This child is destined for the falling and the rising of many in Israel, and to be a sign that will be opposed so that the inner thoughts of many will be revealed—and a sword will pierce your own soul too.'

There was also a prophet, Anna the daughter of Phanuel, of the tribe of Asher. She was of a great age, having lived with her husband for seven years after her marriage, then as a widow to the age of eighty-four. She never left the temple but worshipped there with fasting and prayer night and day. At that moment she came, and began to praise God and to speak about the child to all who were looking for the redemption of Jerusalem.

When they had finished everything required by the law of the Lord, they returned to Galilee, to their own town of Nazareth.

LUKE 2:22–39

Following Jesus' circumcision, Mary and Joseph continue to be fully obedient to the Jewish law. Thirty-three days later, when Mary's purification is complete, the child is brought to be presented to the Lord in the temple in Jerusalem (Leviticus 12:2–8).

The idea that a woman is rendered impure by virtue of giving birth may strike us as odd. However, in today's reading Mary's 'impurity' is important because it signifies the true humanity of both herself and the Christ-child. This is a birth within Judaism just like any other, and both Mary and her baby submit to the rules and regulations of the Jewish law. How remarkable that the eternal Word through whom the universe was made should be so humble!

In some ways it is a pity that the Christian rite of 'The Thanksgiving of Women after Childbirth' is rarely practised nowadays. Perhaps people are put off by its other title, 'The Churching of Women'. This was a service of thanksgiving for the preservation of the mother and safe delivery of the child. Of course, childbirth was much more dangerous in the past, but it can still be hazardous today, so it makes sense to give thanks to God when all turns out well. Extra thanks to God can be given for the gift of modern medicine, which has made vast strides in limiting maternal mortality, although we also need to pray that the benefits we enjoy in the West will be extended to lower-income countries around the world where pregnancy remains as dangerous as ever. It is sobering to think that in Britain the maternal mortality rate is about twelve deaths per year per 100,000 live births, but in Somalia about 1000 mothers die per 100,000 live births.

The normal offering that a woman brought to the priest when her purification was complete was a lamb plus a turtle-dove or pigeon. However, for the poor, like Mary and Joseph, a pair of turtledoves or pigeons was allowed as an alternative.

In the temple, the holy family encounter two more devout Jews, Simeon and Anna. These two old people were among the expectant 'quiet in the land' (Psalm 35:20), who spent all the time they could in the temple, worshipping, fasting and praying. Each of them was longing, waiting and believing that Israel's hopes would soon be fulfilled, and each saw that these hopes were now being realised in the child Jesus.

Inspired by the Holy Spirit, Simeon had had a revelation that he would see the Messiah before he died. The same Spirit inspired his wonderful song, which we know as the Nunc Dimittis (vv. 29–32). It is sung at Evensong and quite often, and very appropriately, at funerals.

Simeon knew he could die in peace because he had seen the Lord's Christ. Simeon's song tells us that the salvation Christ brings is not just for his Jewish compatriots but for all peoples. This is exactly what the prophets had foretold. For example, in Deutero-Isaiah's second servant song, God says, 'It is too light a thing that you should be my servant to raise up the tribes of Jacob and to restore the survivors of Israel; I will give you as a light to the nations, that my salvation may reach to the end of the earth' (Isaiah 49:6).

Simeon's message to Mary is about the division that her child will cause. Scholars debate whether Simeon meant that the same people would fall, then rise, or that one group would fall and another rise. Either way, Jesus' message would be rejected by many, even if a large number later repented of being complicit in Jesus' death (Acts 2:37). It is sad, though, that the gospel message of God's love for all, and the offer of salvation to all, should be rejected by anyone. Simeon seemed to understand where this would all lead. The shadow of the cross hung over Jesus even in his early infancy. Understandably, this would have the effect of a sword piercing Mary's soul.

The prophetess Anna is one of the many significant women who feature in Luke's Gospel and its sequel, the Acts of the Apostles. Like Simeon's, her life of devotion is crowned by seeing the Lord's Christ. She thanks God and tells 'all who were looking for the redemption of Jerusalem' (v. 38). Those words bring to mind Isaiah 52:9: 'For the Lord has comforted his people, he has redeemed Jerusalem.' As God brought the captives out of Babylon and back to Jerusalem, so he brings about the full and final return from exile for all sinners through Jesus.

I think there are lessons here for our own devotion. Are

we faithful in prayer and worship, as Simeon and Anna were? Is the church our second home, as the temple was for them? Are we listening to God and discerning what his plans are here and now? Anna and Simeon recognised the Saviour of the world in the infant Christ. I trust that we do, too. Having the whole of the gospel story before us, I trust that we recognise how our salvation has been brought about by what followed in Jesus' life, death and resurrection. Like Simeon and Anna, let us praise God for the gift beyond price of his Son and share with others the wonderful good news of the salvation he brings.

For reflection

Ask yourself the following questions.

- *Am I faithful in daily private prayer?*
- *Which helps me most—extempore prayers or set prayers? If my prayer life is feeling stale, would it be helpful to vary my routine?*
- *Do I join other Christians in worship on Sundays, no matter where I am?*
- *Am I listening to God and discerning his plans?*

Take time to examine your devotion to God, and resolve, with the help of the Holy Spirit, to draw closer to him.

Living Christ's ethically radical way

'You have heard that it was said to those of ancient times, "You shall not murder"; and "whoever murders shall be liable to judgement." But I say to you that if you are angry with a brother or sister, you will be liable to judgement; and if you insult a brother or sister, you will be liable to the council; and if you say, "You fool", you will be liable to the hell of fire. So when you are offering your gift at the altar, if you remember that your brother or sister has something against you, leave your gift there before the altar and go; first be reconciled to your brother or sister, and then come and offer your gift. Come to terms quickly with your accuser while you are on the way to court with him, or your accuser may hand you over to the judge, and the judge to the guard, and you will be thrown into prison. Truly I tell you, you will never get out until you have paid the last penny.

'You have heard that it was said, "You shall not commit adultery." But I say to you that everyone who looks at a woman with lust has already committed adultery with her in his heart. If your right eye causes you to sin, tear it out and throw it away; it is better for you to lose one of your members than for your whole body to be thrown into hell.

And if your right hand causes you to sin, cut it off and throw
it away; it is better for you to lose one of your members than
for your whole body to go into hell.'
MATTHEW 5:21–30

The Sermon on the Mount, from which today's passage is an
extract, is at the heart of Jesus' radical teaching on how his
disciples should behave to others. It is full of graphic imagery,
as well as seemingly impossible demands that, at best, we can
only hope to aspire to.

It would seem that our eternal destiny is decided by how
we match up to these impossible demands. The person who
calls his brother or sister 'You fool' is liable to 'the hell of fire'.
Our worship and our giving cannot be considered genuine
if our brother or sister has something against us and we
remain unreconciled to him or her. Similarly, the one who
has lustful thoughts is condemned, let alone someone who
puts such thoughts into practice. The person whose eye or
hand causes him or her to sin should resort to self-mutilation
to avoid hell. Jesus isn't abolishing the law here; he is telling
us what it really means. To be angry with a brother or sister,
or to insult him or her, is to disobey the command, 'You shall
not kill', and to look lustfully on a woman is to disobey the
command, 'You shall not commit adultery'. We are to love
our brothers and sisters in purity of word and thought.

The popular perception is that, when we die, we go either
to heaven or to hell. At best, this is a rather naïve picture in
both cases. The destiny of the just is to an embodied future
life on a renewed earth (see 5 January). The word 'hell',
which is used infrequently in the New Testament, translates
two different words. One is the Greek *Hades*, which is used to
translate the Hebrew word *Sheol* in the Greek version of the

Old Testament. The other is the Hebrew word *Gehenna*. In today's passage, the word used is *Gehenna*, which denotes the smouldering rubbish dump, the valley of the son of Hinnom, which runs round the west and south sides of Jerusalem. It was used for child sacrifice in Old Testament times (see, for example, 2 Chronicles 33:6).

It is not surprising that we get our images of hell-fire from so graphic a real-life picture, and it is typical of Jesus to use an image like this from everyday life—an image that would be well-known to his listeners. And surely it is just that—an image, picture language, as any kind of description of what happens after death must be. The main point must be that those who do evil bring upon themselves banishment from God's presence (Matthew 7:23; 2 Thessalonians 1:9) (see 19 and 20 December on the possibility that some will persist in saying 'no' to God).

A worrying thought is that our behaviour makes us all worthy of hell, since Jesus' standards are impossible to meet. Thankfully, not many Christians have taken literally the instruction to tear out an eye or cut off a hand. As Bonhoeffer says in commenting on this passage, to ask whether Jesus is speaking literally or only figuratively is to ask the wrong question. The real question is, are we taking Jesus' commandment with the utmost seriousness that it requires?

Bonhoeffer rightly sees that the only way we can meet these commands is by looking at Jesus first and foremost. Jesus bore the worst of insults on our behalf. He is our crucified brother and we are to imitate him. To look on him is to be 'succoured with the grace of the gospel'.[40] It is only by grace that we can become like him and act towards others in the way he commands. One important conclusion from this is that we cannot judge others (Matthew 7:1–5). We cannot say of any person that he or she is beyond redemption, because by Christ's own criteria we are all failures.

Jesus does, however, really intend that his disciples will adopt a radically different way of acting in the world from accepted norms, and he will enable the Christian to follow this 'more excellent way', as Paul describes it (1 Corinthians 12:31). We are to obey the 'golden rule': 'In everything do to others as you would have them do to you.' Jesus uses this phrase to summarise all his teaching in the Sermon on the Mount (Matthew 7:12). In today's extract, we are instructed to be reconciled with our brother or sister and to have pure thoughts. Jesus requires us in the rest of chapter 5 to make marriage a lifelong commitment, to be utterly truthful without the need to swear, and not to take revenge but, on the contrary, to 'turn the other cheek' and 'go the extra mile'. We are not to love our neighbour and hate our enemy but to love our enemies. As Jesus rightly says, to love one's friends is simply the normal, done thing—'even the tax collectors' do that. But his disciples must be perfect, as their heavenly Father is perfect (5:48). This is the blueprint for the kingdom of God, which begins to take shape as Jesus' disciples start to act by his radical new ethic.

For reflection

To live in Christ's ethically radical way, we need God's grace throughout the day. It is therefore very important to turn aside often to him, to stop and be still for a few moments. You might like to try to make the following your own daily practice. Stop to seek the free gift of God's grace and his help for whatever you are doing or whoever you are seeing or serving or meeting:

- *Hold your hands together before you, palms upwards.*
- *Wait in silence, reminding yourself that God is with you.*
- *Ask him to pour into your hands his gift of grace and help.*

Children and heirs

My point is this: heirs, as long as they are minors, are no better than slaves, though they are the owners of all the property; but they remain under guardians and trustees until the date set by the father. So with us; while we were minors, we were enslaved to the elemental spirits of the world. But when the fullness of time had come, God sent his Son, born of a woman, born under the law, in order to redeem those who were under the law, so that we might receive adoption as children. And because you are children, God has sent the Spirit of his Son into our hearts, crying, 'Abba! Father!' So you are no longer a slave but a child, and if a child then also an heir, through God.

Formerly, when you did not know God, you were enslaved to beings that by nature are not gods. Now, however, that you have come to know God, or rather to be known by God, how can you turn back again to the weak and beggarly elemental spirits? How can you want to be enslaved to them again? You are observing special days, and months, and seasons, and years. I am afraid that my work for you may have been wasted.

GALATIANS 4:1–11

The Galatian Christians to whom Paul is writing are being tempted either to go back to Judaism if they are Jews, or to embrace Jewish observances if they are Gentiles. In his letter Paul upbraids them in the harshest terms for being so perverse: 'You foolish Galatians! Who has bewitched you? (3:1).

Before becoming Christians, the Jews were 'under the law'. This meant they had to observe a great collection of rules and regulations, and Paul probably has three especially in mind—circumcision, the food laws and observance of the sabbath. He compares this submission to the law to a situation where a young son and heir is under the care of guardians. Until he grows up and comes into his inheritance, the son is no better than a slave.

The Jews would have been astonished to be put in the same boat as the Gentiles! Paul equates being under the law of Moses to being 'enslaved to the elemental spirits of the world' (4:3). What are these 'elemental spirits'? Well, one possible meaning of the term is the physical elements that combine to make all things, which, to the Greeks, were fire, air, water and earth. We now know the real elements to be those of the periodic table—hydrogen, helium, lithium, beryllium and so on. It is these that combine to make all material objects, but the Greeks had at least made a stab at the truth with their four basic elements.

The first-century Jewish writer Philo tells us, however, that the Greeks gave the four elements the names of gods. He rightly says that these elements have no power of their own since they are just inanimate matter. Likewise, the things made out of them—the sun, moon, stars and planets, which the Greeks also worshipped as gods—do not exist of their own accord but owe their existence entirely to the Creator.[41] The Jews, like Philo, thought they knew better than the Greeks, because they knew that the elements and the heavenly bodies were merely objects created by God to give them light

(Genesis 1:16). So it would have come as totally shocking to be told that being under the law, or reverting to the law, was the same as being in thrall to the star-gods. Similarly, many people in our society today have turned their back on God and are in thrall to their horoscopes.

Jews and Gentiles are thus in the same position. However, over these last few weeks we have been celebrating the fact that 'when the fullness of time had come, God sent his Son, born of a woman, born under the law, in order to redeem those who were under the law' (vv. 4–5). Jesus' birth came at just the right moment in history—and, particularly, in salvation history. The rule of law had done its job and the time was right for the freedom of grace.

Through Jesus, the Son of God by nature, eternally begotten of the Father before all worlds, we become adopted as children of God, and heirs. As a result of Jesus' death and resurrection, we have received the Holy Spirit in our hearts, who cries, 'Abba! Father!' (v. 6). What an amazing privilege and how liberating it is to be able to call God 'Father'! It is equally special that Jesus encourages us to use the Aramaic word *Abba*, used originally by children speaking to their earthly father. This is the intimate family word for 'father' and, by the time Paul is writing, it was also being used by adults to address their father. It was never used, however, by Jews addressing their prayers to God, so the use of the word *Abba* shows the wonderful new, intimate relationship with God into which we have been brought by Christ.

Paul is critical of the Galatians' observing days, months, seasons and years. It would seem that Gentile converts as well as Jews were using the Jewish calendar. Since the times and seasons were determined by the sun, moon and stars (Genesis 1:14), perhaps the Gentiles were being encouraged in the belief that the heavenly bodies were gods.

The question for us is, are we enslaved to any worldly or material influences, or even to the heavenly bodies? Are we bound by rules and regulations? I trust we don't read horoscopes, but there can be more insidious forms of slavery. Some churches have invented rules and regulations which seem to imply that Christians have to be miserable—for example, you mustn't go to the cinema; you mustn't have a glass of wine; you must be very strict about what you do on a Sunday. They seem to forget that Jesus was criticised for being a partygoer and for breaking the sabbath. Of course we mustn't go to the other extreme and think that anything goes (Paul puts this balancing side of the argument in 1 Corinthians 6:12–20), but let's enjoy the wonderful, gracious gift of freedom that we have been given as children of the living God. As children and heirs, let us cry to God in joy and praise, 'Abba! Father!'

For reflection

My baptismal birthday
God's child in Christ adopted—Christ my all—
What that earth boasts were not lost cheaply, rather
Than forfeit that blest name, by which I call
The holy One, the Almighty God, my Father?—
Father! in Christ we live, and Christ in Thee—
Eternal Thou, and everlasting we.
The heir of heaven, henceforth I fear not death:
In Christ I live! in Christ I draw the breath
Of the true life!—Let, then, earth, sea, and sky
Make war against me! On my front I show
Their mighty Master's seal. In vain they try

To end my life, that can but end its woe—
Is that a deathbed where a Christian lies?—
Yes! but not his—'tis Death itself that dies.

SAMUEL TAYLOR COLERIDGE

Heaven on earth

I saw no temple in the city, for its temple is the Lord God the Almighty and the Lamb. And the city has no need of sun or moon to shine on it, for the glory of God is its light, and its lamp is the Lamb. The nations will walk by its light, and the kings of the earth will bring their glory into it. Its gates will never be shut by day—and there will be no night there. People will bring into it the glory and the honour of the nations. But nothing unclean will enter it, nor anyone who practises abomination or falsehood, but only those who are written in the Lamb's book of life.

Then the angel showed me the river of the water of life, bright as crystal, flowing from the throne of God and of the Lamb through the middle of the street of the city. On either side of the river is the tree of life with its twelve kinds of fruit, producing its fruit each month; and the leaves of the tree are for the healing of the nations. Nothing accursed will be found there any more. But the throne of God and of the Lamb will be in it, and his servants will worship him; they will see his face, and his name will be on their foreheads. And there will be no more night; they need no light of lamp or sun, for the Lord God will be their light, and they will reign for ever and ever.

REVELATION 21:22—22:5

John gives us a wonderful picture of the final consummation of all things. This is what Christ came into the world to bring about—the new heavens and the new earth in which 'Death will be no more; mourning and crying and pain will be no more, for the first things have passed away' (Revelation 21:4). Jesus is the first fruits, and our ultimate destiny is to share in his new resurrection life. This is what we have been longing and waiting for and what we believe will come to pass because Jesus, in dying and rising again, unites us with himself (Romans 6:5–8).

We often talk loosely about 'going to heaven' when we die, and we imagine heaven to be 'up there', but this isn't the language that scripture uses. Indeed, in the book of Revelation, the opposite happens: the heavenly city, the new Jerusalem, comes down to us, and this physical creation is renewed. Like the last judgement, this can only be expressed in picture language. One indication that the renewal is of our present earth is that the heavenly city is constructed from the precious stones of *this* creation (21:18–21). Moreover, 'people will bring into it the glory and the honour of the nations' (v. 26).

There are many echoes of the Old Testament in today's passage. The temple was God's dwelling place, although even Solomon who built it recognised that 'heaven and the highest heaven cannot contain you, much less this house that I have built!' (1 Kings 8:27). This was a truth that the Israelites had to learn the hard way. Temple worship became corrupt and the temple was eventually destroyed. The exiles in Babylon had to realise that God was to be found there too, in the midst of their sorrow and desolation (see Ezekiel's vision in Ezekiel 1). In Jesus' day, the second temple was also corrupt, and it was finally destroyed by the Romans in AD70. However, in the new Jerusalem there will be no need of a physical temple because God himself will be its temple.

In the creation story, God separates the light from the darkness and provides two great lights to rule them. In the new Jerusalem, there will be no need for sun and moon, because 'the glory of God is its light, and its lamp is the Lamb' (21:23). Here again are echoes of Jesus' words, 'I am the light of the world' (John 8:12).

In the new Jerusalem it will be permanently 'day'; there will be no night or darkness. This is spelled out by what follows in Revelation 21: 'Nothing unclean will enter it, nor anyone who practises abomination or falsehood' (v. 27). Everyone there will follow the light—the way of love, truth, peace and harmony—but we are warned that those who do not follow the light will be excluded and 'only those who are written in the Lamb's book of life' will enter. Again, let me say that those excluded from the city will be consciously self-selected and self-willed. Sadly, love may just be too much for some people to take.

Further Old Testament allusions follow. The 'water of life' (22:1) brings to mind the visions of Ezekiel 47 and Zechariah 14:8, in which living waters flow out from the restored Jerusalem temple. Jesus brings these visions to fruition, for he embodies the temple in his own person, having said, 'Destroy this temple, and in three days I will raise it up' (John 2:19–21). In John 7:37–38 Jesus appropriates Isaiah 55:1 to himself, with the invitation 'Let anyone who is thirsty come to me, and let the one who believes in me drink', and promises that living waters will flow out of the heart of the one who believes in him. This water represents the Holy Spirit, as did the water that flowed from Jesus' side when he was pierced with a sword on the cross (John 19:34).

The 'tree of life' stood in the midst of the garden of Eden

(Genesis 2:9) and, in the story, Adam and Eve were eventually prevented from eating of it because they had disobeyed God by eating from the tree of the knowledge of good and evil (3:24). Humanity has forfeited the offer of immortality because of sin, but has been graciously given eternal life through the death of the Lamb. The tree of life will stand in the holy city and bear fruit all year round, its leaves being 'for the healing of the nations (Revelation 22:2).

Metaphor is laid on metaphor here, but wonderful truth is being conveyed thereby. Humankind, as symbolised by Adam, forfeited paradise, but a far richer and more glorious paradise has been gained for all by Jesus Christ. Now that's something to celebrate!

For reflection

Love bade me welcome; yet my soul drew back,
Guilty of dust and sin.
But quick-ey'd Love, observing me grow slack
From my first entrance in,
Drew nearer to me, sweetly questioning,
If I lack'd any thing.

'A guest', I answer'd, 'worthy to be here.'
Love said, 'You shall be he.'
'I the unkind, ungrateful? Ah, my dear,
I cannot look on thee.'
Love took my hand, and smiling did reply,
'Who made the eyes but I?'

'Truth, Lord, but I have marr'd them: let my shame
Go where it doth deserve.'

'And know you not', says Love, 'who bore the blame?'
  'My dear, then I will serve.'
'You must sit down', says Love, 'and taste my meat.'
  So I did sit and eat.
GEORGE HERBERT, 'LOVE III'

Journeying in faith

In the time of King Herod, after Jesus was born in Bethlehem of Judea, wise men from the East came to Jerusalem, asking, 'Where is the child who has been born king of the Jews? For we observed his star at its rising, and have come to pay him homage.' When King Herod heard this, he was frightened, and all Jerusalem with him; and calling together all the chief priests and scribes of the people, he inquired of them where the Messiah was to be born. They told him, 'In Bethlehem of Judea; for so it has been written by the prophet:

"And you, Bethlehem, in the land of Judah,
are by no means least among the rulers of Judah;
for from you shall come a ruler
who is to shepherd my people Israel."'

Then Herod secretly called for the wise men and learned from them the exact time when the star had appeared. Then he sent them to Bethlehem, saying, 'Go and search diligently for the child; and when you have found him, bring me word so that I may also go and pay him homage.' When they had heard the king, they set out; and there, ahead of them, went the star that they had seen at its rising, until it stopped over the place where the child was. When they saw that the star had stopped, they were overwhelmed with joy. On entering the house, they saw the child with Mary his mother; and they knelt down and paid him homage. Then, opening their treasure-chests, they offered him gifts of gold, frankincense, and myrrh. And having been warned in a dream not to return to Herod, they left for their own country by another road.

MATTHEW 2:1–12

We end our series of reflections very appropriately with the Epiphany, the manifesting of Christ to the nations. Jesus is at one and the same time the Messiah and King of the Jews *and* the Saviour of the whole world. The Jews, the chosen race, have been, all along, God's vehicle for his purpose of saving the whole of humanity. The gospel is not narrow and nationalistic, but is for everyone.

As with all the New Testament passages we have considered over the last few weeks, there are strong echoes here of the Old Testament, besides the direct quotation from Micah which signifies Bethlehem as the town where the Messiah is to be born (Micah 5:2). There is also the story of Balaam, the foreign seer who was recruited by the Moabite king Balak to curse the Israelites but blessed them instead. Balaam's words, 'a star shall come out of Jacob' (Numbers 24:17), are reflected in the star of Bethlehem, which the magi, seers from the east, see at its rising and follow to find the newborn king.

The reason we call the wise men 'kings' no doubt stems from some of the other scriptural allusions. In Isaiah 60:3 we read, 'Nations shall come to your light, and kings to the brightness of your dawn', and that passage also tells us that gifts of gold and frankincense shall be brought (v. 6). In Psalm 72, foreign kings also bring gifts, including gold (v. 15). Other passages that spring to mind include the queen of Sheba bringing spices and gold to King Solomon, who answers the 'hard questions' with which she tests him (1 Kings 10:1–4).

The magi seem to have some knowledge of what is to happen, from their astronomical observations, but deeper knowledge comes from God's revelation in the Hebrew scriptures. There is an analogy here with the two sources of knowledge of God that theologians have traditionally distinguished. The first is natural knowledge, which we obtain simply by being human. Some of that knowledge can come from science: for example, the way the universe exhibits an ordered structure, which is open to science to investigate, points to a mind behind it. The second source of knowledge is God's revelation, supremely in the person of Jesus Christ, and the holy scriptures are God's revelation because they bear witness to him. This latter source of knowledge is both more detailed and more reliable than the former.

The magi were careful observers of the heavens and would easily have spotted a new star, but they were astrologers rather than astronomers. Astrology would not, under normal circumstances, produce reliable knowledge at all of events on earth. However, God meets us where we are. If a sign will speak to those he wants to reach, God can, if he pleases, give signs in the heavens.

Herod's behaviour is hypocritical, since, as we saw on Holy Innocents' Day, his real intentions are malign. He seems to believe that Micah's prophecy that the Messiah will come from Bethlehem (Micah 5:2) is from God, but arrogantly thinks he can thwart its fulfilment. Herod is a usurper, from Idumaea, and the kingship really belongs to the line of David. We can appreciate why he would be troubled, and how the anxiety of this monster could overcome the constraints of reason, so that he would even attempt to frustrate the purposes of God.

With all its scriptural allusions and the author's keenness to show at every point how Jesus fulfils Old Testament prophecy, Matthew's Gospel has been thought the most Jewish of the Gospels. Also, the earthly ministry of Jesus and his first disciples was almost entirely to the Jews. Yet Matthew begins with Christ's revelation to the Gentiles in the persons of the magi, and ends with the great commission: 'Go therefore and make disciples of all nations, baptising them in the name of the Father and of the Son and of the Holy Spirit, and teaching them to obey everything that I have commanded you. And remember, I am with you always, to the end of the age' (Matthew 28:19–20).

The longing and waiting, not just of the Jewish people but of the Gentiles too, is over: the Saviour of the world has come. We who believe are on an exciting journey of faith as we discover more and more of the immeasurable riches of God's grace and as we are transformed from within, by his Holy Spirit, into his likeness. We cannot help but share this greatest of all good news with others as we bring Christ's love and compassion to a needy world. We shall meet challenges and hardships but we shall not be deterred as we, like Paul, 'press on towards the goal for the prize of the heavenly call of God in Christ Jesus' (Philippians 3:14).

For reflection

You have journeyed through Advent and Christmas to the Feast of the Epiphany, but your journey does not end here. Will you, like the wise men of old, keep watchful for signs from God, guiding you to see where he is at work in those around you? You might like to write a prayer of dedication for the exciting journey of faith that lies ahead of you.

Questions for reflection and discussion

The following questions can be used by individuals or small groups. The questions are based on the week's Bible readings. If all members of a group have read each day's material, the discussion will be more fruitful. Questions for 21–25 December could be included in the next week's discussion if a group does not meet that week. In advance of the section entitled 'The cost of believing', it would be helpful if someone could investigate organisations that support Christians being persecuted around the world—for example, The Barnabas Fund (www.barnabasfund.org) or Christian Solidarity Worldwide (www.csw.org.uk).

1–6 December: Following God's call

1. The patriarchs heard God's call and followed him. How has God spoken to you through this set of readings?
2. What will it mean for you to 'put on the armour of light' as we pray in the Advent Collect?
3. Where is God for your church community?
4. 'In Christ God was reconciling the world to himself, not counting their trespasses against them, and entrusting the message of reconciliation to us' (2 Corinthians 5:19). What roles of reconciliation should you be taking for those around you?

5. If you are in a group, share in pairs your faith journey and try to reflect back to your partner where God seems to have been working out his purposes.

Close your time by lighting a candle and waiting on God in the quietness or as you listen to some suitable music.

7–13 December: Foretelling God's plan

1. Could you purchase more Fairtrade goods and locally produced food? Could you encourage your church to be a Fairtrade church?
2. 'I will put my law within them' (Jeremiah 31:33). Do you need to study the Bible or can you just rely on God's Spirit to show you what God wants?
3. Who are you, or who could you be, shepherding? How might you become more Christ-like in your caring?
4. What needs to be included in a summary of the good news? Why not make some notes so that you are ready when God gives you an opportunity to share your faith?
5. How will God judge your response to others who are oppressed?

Close your time by lighting a candle and meditating on Philippians 2:3–11.

14–20 December: Turning to God's way

1. 'Prepare the way of the Lord, make his paths straight.' What in your life, or the life of your church or community, should be straightened out for the Lord? Is there anything you can do about it?

2. We all like to do important tasks and be noticed, yet, in our churches, there are many thankless tasks that have to be done. How could you help out with these?
3. As Christmas approaches, how can you point others to Christ? Could you, perhaps, take someone to a service, babysit so that a busy mum can shop in peace, or make lots of mince pies for an old people's home or local hostel or prison?
4. What causes people to doubt God's love? How can doubts be overcome?
5. Look at the verses mentioned on 20 December (Romans 5:18; 2 Corinthians 5:14–15, 19; Titus 2:11; 1 John 2:2; Matthew 18:14; 1 Timothy 2:4; 2 Peter 3:9; Colossians 1:20; Matthew 25:31–46). Consider whether all people will be saved or only some.

Close your time by lighting a candle and reading 1 Corinthians 15:51–58. Then slowly pass a cross round the group. As you give the cross to the next person, look at them and say confidently, 'The trumpet will sound, and we will be changed.'

21–25 December: Welcoming God's Son

1. How can the church as a Christ-bearing community, or you as an individual Christ-bearer, take Christ into the world?
2. Mary and Joseph dared to believe the promises of God. Do you dare to believe that God can transform people's lives, 'even' the lives of those of whom you tend to think the worst?
3. What are you doing for the poor and homeless this Christmas and into the new year?

Close your time by lighting a candle and reading these words, attributed to Teresa of Avila:

Christ has no body now on earth but yours,
no hands but yours, no feet but yours,
Yours are the eyes through which to look out
Christ's compassion to the world;
Yours are the feet with which he is to go about doing good;
Yours are the hands with which he is to bless men now.

26–29 December: The cost of believing

1. Do you think the rights of Christians in Britain are being infringed? Have you come across opposition to your faith? How should Christians react to opposition and persecution?
2. How can you become better informed about Christians who are being persecuted around the world? What can you do individually and as a church to support them? (Organisations that resource persecuted Christians include The Barnabas Fund, www.barnabasfund.org, and Christian Solidarity Worldwide, www.csw.org.uk.)
3. 'The commandment we have from him is this: those who love God must love their brothers and sisters also' (1 John 4:21). Who are these brothers and sisters?

Close your time by lighting a candle and praying for Christians who are facing persecution.

30 December–6 January: Living in the 'now and not yet'

1. Paul wrote to Timothy, 'from childhood you have known the sacred writings' (2 Timothy 3:15). What can you do to encourage children to get to know the Bible? If you are not in contact with children directly, could you support Bible Society or another organisation?
2. The shepherds 'made known what had been told them about this child' (Luke 2:17). Do you keep your faith to yourself or do you share it with others? Can you discern where God's Spirit is at work in your community and where you can join in the adventure of forthtelling?
3. Jesus' ethical teaching requires self-control and thought-control. How can you practise these virtues? Does Paul's advice help: 'Set your minds on things that are above, not on things that are on earth' (Colossians 3:2)?
4. Are you bound by any habitual practices or enslaved to any worldly values?
5. 'I can do all things through him who strengthens me' (Philippians 4:13). What are you looking forward to doing in God's strength as you continue your journey with him?

Notes

1   Collect for Advent Sunday, *Common Worship: Services and Prayers for the Church of England* (Church House Publishing, 2000), p. 376.

2   Josephus, *Antiquities of the Jews*, 1.12.3, in William Whiston (trans.), *The Works of Josephus* (Hendrickson, 1987), p. 42.

3   Adapted from *Helps to Worship: A manual for Holy Communion and daily prayer*, dedicated by permission to the Lord Bishop of Oxford by two of his priests (Charles T. Boyd and H.G.J. Meara) (Mowbray, 1877), pp. 22–23.

4   Anthony Tyrell Hanson, *The Wrath of the Lamb* (SPCK, 1957), p. 160.

5   Eberhard Bethge, *Dietrich Bonhoeffer: Theologian, Christian, Contemporary* (Collins, 1970), p. 511.

6   Karl Barth, *Church Dogmatics*, IV/1 (T&T Clark, 1956), §59.2, 'The Judge judged in our place', pp. 211–283.

7   N.T. Wright, *Jesus and the Victory of God* (SPCK, 1996), p. 127.

8   Jürgen Moltmann, *The Crucified God*, trans. R.A. Wilson and John Bowden (SCM, 1974). See especially pp. 147–155, 286–288.

9   Josephus, *Antiquities*, 18.5.2, in Whiston, *Works of Josephus*, p. 484.

10 Richard Holloway, *Leaving Alexandria: A memoir of faith and doubt* (Canongate, 2013).

11 Dietrich Bonhoeffer, *Letters and Papers from Prison*, enlarged edn, ed. Eberhard Bethge (SCM, 1971), p. 337.

12 Bethge, *Dietrich Bonhoeffer*, p. 830.

13 John Bunyan, *The Pilgrim's Progress* Part 2 (Penguin Classics, 2008), p. 311.

14 C.S. Lewis, *The Great Divorce* (Geoffrey Bles, 1946), pp. 66–67.

15 'Papa Panov's Special Christmas', in Mary Bachelor (comp.), *The Lion Christmas Book* (Lion, 1984), p. 84.

16 Opening prayer of thanks for Advent at Morning Prayer, *Common Worship: Daily Prayer* (Church House Publishing, 2005), p. 198.

17 These include Romans 5:18; 2 Corinthians 5:14–15, 19; Titus 2:11; 1 John 2:2.

18 For example, Matthew 18:14; 1 Timothy 2:4; 2 Peter 3:9.

19 Lewis, *Great Divorce*, pp. 114–115.

20 C.S. Lewis, *The Last Battle* (Bodley Head, 1956).

21 Miroslav Volf, *Exclusion and Embrace* (Abingdon Press, 1996), p. 298.

22 Dietrich Bonhoeffer, 'Ethics as Formation', in *Ethics* I.III (Collins, 1964), p. 83.

23 Thomas Aquinas, *Summa Theologiae*, 1a, 105.5.

24 Aquinas, *Summa Theologiae*, 1a, 105.6.

25 N.T. Wright, *Jesus and the Victory of God* (SPCK, 1996), pp. 186–187, footnote.

26 From a Tearfund Christmas collection of poems and Bible studies.

27 The Third Letter of Cyril to Nestorius, in E.R. Hardy (ed.), *Christology of the Later Fathers*, Library of Christian Classics Vol. III (SCM, 1954), p. 350.

28 'Nativity', in John Donne, *The Major Works*, Oxford World Classics edition (Oxford University Press, 2000), pp. 171–172.

29 See Philippians 2:15; also 2 Corinthians 3:18, where the translation 'reflecting the glory of the Lord' is to be preferred to 'seeing the glory of the Lord as though reflected in a mirror'.

30. Dietrich Bonhoeffer, *The Cost of Discipleship*, first German edn as *Nachfolge*, 1937 (SCM, 1959), pp. 79, 80–81.

31. Richard Bauckham, *Jesus and the Eyewitnesses: The Gospels as eyewitness testimony* (Eerdmans, 2006), ch. 14.

32. Josephus, *Antiquities*, 16.5.4, in Whiston, *Works of Josephus*, p. 435.

33. From Winston Churchill, 'This was their finest hour', speech to the House of Commons, 18 June 1940.

34. Rowan Williams, *Dostoevsky: Language, faith and fiction* (Continuum, 2009).

35. Dietrich Bonhoeffer, *Creation and Fall: A theological exposition of Genesis 1—3*, English edition, ed. John W. de Gruchy, trans. D.S. Bax (Fortress Press, 1997), p. 35.

36. Bonhoeffer, *Letters and Papers from Prison* ed. Bethge, pp. 381, 370.

37. Adapted from 'How to pray for persecuted Christians', a prayer bookmark published by Barnabas Fund. © Barnabas Fund, 2012, www.barnabasfund.org

38. 'A sonnet for Corpus Christi' in Malcolm Guite, *Sounding the Seasons: Seventy sonnets for the Christian year* (Canterbury Press, 2012), p. 49.

39. Collect for Last Sunday after Trinity, *Common Worship: Services and Prayers for the Church of England*, p. 422. In the Book of Common Prayer it is the Collect for the Second Sunday in Advent.

40 Bonhoeffer, *Cost of Discipleship*, p. 120.

41 Philo, *On the Contemplative Life*, 3–4, in trans. C.D. Yonge, *The Works of Philo* (Hendrickson, 1993), p. 698.

Reflecting the Glory

Bible readings and reflections
for Lent and Easter

Tom Wright

You can't love an abstraction. You can't even love the idea of love. You can only truly love a person. The relevance of knowing God in Jesus is that when we love God in Jesus we discover how that love, that personal love, is given to us in order that it may be given through us.

This book of Bible readings and reflections, for every day from Ash Wednesday to the first Sunday of Easter, explores how we reveal Jesus even at the lowest and weakest points of our lives. Drawing on New Testament passages, with a particular focus on Paul's letters to the church in Corinth, Tom Wright shows that through God's Holy Spirit, the suffering but also the glory of Christ can be incarnate in our lives, enabling us to be the people of God for the world.

ISBN 978 0 7459 3556 0   £8.99

Available from your local Christian bookshop or direct from BRF: visit www.brfonline.org.uk

ENJOYED READING THIS
ADVENT BOOK?

Did you know BRF publishes a new Lent and Advent book each year? All
our Lent and Advent books are designed with a daily printed Bible reading,
comment and reflection. Some can be used in groups and contain questions
which can be used in a study or reading group.

Previous Advent books have included:

Real God in the Real World, Trystan Owain Hughes
Companions on the Bethlehem Road, Rachel Boulding
The Incredible Journey, Steve Brady
Pilgrims to the Manger, Naomi Starkey

> If you would like to be kept in touch with information about our
> forthcoming Lent or Advent books, please complete the coupon below.

✂- -

❏ Please keep me in touch by post with forthcoming Lent or Advent books
❏ Please email me with details about forthcoming Lent or Advent books

Email address: _____

Name _____

Address_____

_____

_____

Postcode _____

Telephone_____

Signature _____

**Please send this
completed form to:**

Freepost RRLH-JCYA-SZX
BRF, 15 The Chambers,
Vineyard, Abingdon,
OX14 3FE, United Kingdom

Tel. 01865 319700
Fax. 01865 319701
Email: enquiries@brf.org.uk

www.brf.org.uk

PROMO REF: END/ADVENT14

BRF is a Registered Charity

For more information, visit the **brf** website at **www.brf.org.uk**